Selected Poems

NORTHWESTERN WORLD CLASSICS

Northwestern World Classics brings readers
the world's greatest literature. The series features
essential new editions of well-known works,
lesser-known books that merit reconsideration,
and lost classics of fiction, drama, and poetry.
Insightful commentary and compelling new translations
help readers discover the joy of outstanding writing
from all regions of the world.

Vladimir Mayakovsky

Selected Poems

Translated from the Russian by James H. McGavran III

Northwestern University Press ✦ *Evanston, Illinois*

Northwestern University Press
www.nupress.northwestern.edu

Printed in the United States of America

10 9 8 7 6 5 4 3 2 1

Library of Congress Cataloging-in-Publication Data

Mayakovsky, Vladimir, 1893–1930.
   [Poems. English. Selections]
   Vladimir Mayakovsky : selected poems / translated from the
Russian by James H. McGavran III.
      p. cm. — (Northwestern world classics)
   ISBN 978-0-8101-2907-8 (pbk. : alk. paper)
   1. Mayakovsky, Vladimir, 1893–1930—Translations into English.
I. McGavran, James Holt, 1979– II. Title. III. Series: Northwestern
world classics.
PG3476.M3A2 2013
891.7142—dc23

                                        2012049697

CONTENTS

Much of my work on this collection was completed when I was a Mellon postdoctoral fellow in Russian at Kenyon College, and I am grateful to the Mellon Foundation and the Department of Modern Languages and Literatures at Kenyon for this opportunity. At Kenyon, Katherine Hedeen and Víctor Rodríguez-Núñez offered kind and useful advice when I was still looking for a publisher for my translations. Natalia Olshanskaya, whom I have been most fortunate to count as a mentor, advocate, and friend since my undergraduate days, provided invaluable input on my translations and introduction, as well as support and professional advice throughout my time at Kenyon.

Michael Wachtel, my dissertation adviser at Princeton University, reviewed an early draft of my introduction and made a number of helpful suggestions. I also take this opportunity to acknowledge his unflagging support and guidance as I made the transition from graduate school to the beginning of an academic career.

I am grateful to Michael Levine at Northwestern University Press for his early championing of my project and his prompt answers to questions big and small throughout my work on it. Xenia Lisanevich and Anne Gendler did an excellent job editing my manuscript, and Marianne Jankowski oversaw the design of a beautiful cover featuring artwork by Mayakovsky.

I thank my parents, Dorothy and Jim McGavran, for the material support, sage advice, and loving encouragement that saw me through college and graduate school (not to mention the years before and since).

My greatest debt of gratitude is to my wife, Cherie Braden. She is my front-line and last-line editor, my arbiter of good taste, and my ultimate authority on the English language, and her careful readings and rereadings of my introduction, translations, and notes have improved them in more ways than I can enumerate here.

Vladimir Mayakovsky was first and foremost a poet, to hear him tell it (see the opening words of his autobiography, "I Myself"), but his life and career choices would make it difficult for readers and critics to remain focused on that primary and primal vocation. Indeed, Mayakovsky himself lost sight of it at times and actively repressed his poetic gift at others, but he found that he could never quite escape it. As he wrote in the 1924 poem "Jubilee," "poetry's / the damnedest thing: // it exists— / and we can't make heads or tails of it."[1] He studied painting before he ever wrote a line of verse, working as a visual artist at various points throughout his life. He wrote and acted in plays and films (almost always playing some version of himself), published numerous articles and essays, and worked as an ad man for state-run stores and trusts in the mid-1920s. After the Bolshevik Revolution of October 1917, which he wholeheartedly supported, Mayakovsky devoted himself to serving the new Soviet state through propaganda and patriotic verse, and it is this choice—no one forced him to do it—that turned him, his oeuvre, and his legacy into the battlefield they remain to this day. One hundred years after his first publication, Mayakovsky the poet is still fighting to be understood.

Because the bulk of his output before the Revolution was on lyrical themes and the bulk of his postrevolutionary verse was political, it is easy and perhaps inevitable to compartmentalize his career, or even to speak of two Mayakovskys—such talk began while the poet was still alive, and it became a sort of critical orthodoxy after Stalin's enshrinement of him in 1935 (as we shall see in the following section). The dichotomy, however, is a false one, and we must look past it to understand Mayakovsky's achievements as a poet. His linguistic eccentric-

ity and verve, his ear for powerful rhythms and innovative, se-
mantically loaded rhymes, his mastery of metaphor, and his
irrepressible creative whimsy can all be traced through his
most personal lyrics and his most strident propaganda. In-
deed, his propaganda is at times startlingly personal in its ex-
ecution, and the carryover of larger themes and conflicts from
his lyrical to his political verse lends resonance to both. The
search for a holistic, integrated understanding of Mayakovsky
is nothing new. In a sense, it is the fundamental challenge he
bequeathed to all his readers and critics, and it is a challenge
many have accepted. As early as 1931 (one year after the poet's
suicide), Roman Jakobson wrote, "The poetry of Mayakovsky
from his first verses . . . to his last lines is one and indivisible.
It represents the dialectical development of a single theme. It
is an extraordinarily unified symbolic system."[2] Unfortunately,
the unity Jakobson saw in his friend's oeuvre—the two men
were close, though Jakobson emigrated in 1920—was largely
ignored for the next several decades as more divisive inter-
pretations came to the fore; the poet Jakobson knew was swal-
lowed up by the manufactured legend of an ideologically pure,
revolutionary warrior. Later scholars, however, have renewed
the search for Mayakovsky's thematic and symbolic unity and
taken it in fascinating directions, particularly in the two de-
cades since the fall of the Soviet Union.

If it was Mayakovsky's creative and career choices that opened
the door to ideological interpretations of his verse, it was Sta-
lin who institutionalized the one-sided, political approach to
his work. Stalin drafted the following resolution in red pencil
directly on top of a letter from Lily Brik: "Mayakovsky was and
remains the best and most talented poet of our Soviet epoch.
Indifference to his memory and his works is a crime."[3] Brik
had written to Stalin on November 24, 1935, to complain of
the officially sanctioned oblivion into which Mayakovsky had

fallen since his death.[4] Why Stalin even considered Brik's appeal, much less reacted so affirmatively to it, remains a source of speculation. The central point to be made from the standpoint of Mayakovsky's critical legacy is that Stalin's praise was not based on aesthetic judgment, or on any appreciation of Mayakovsky's poetry as poetry. State poets can be useful to a totalitarian regime, but living poets are dangerously unpredictable. A dead poet, on the other hand, can be molded to serve the regime's purposes through aggressive marketing and education—propaganda in the guise of literary criticism. Still, it does seem odd that a more suitable candidate for the position of Soviet Poet #1 could not be found, and one can marvel at the fantastic irony of enshrining such an iconoclastic poet, a man who was so explicitly contemptuous of what he saw as bourgeois public veneration and "textbook lacquer."[5]

In terms of legacy and critical reputation, Stalin's categorical and ominous praise has been seen by many as a kiss of death, the precedent for what would become one of the two Soviet protocols for ruining an artist: the firing squad and the Stalin Prize. As Boris Pasternak wrote in an oft-cited passage on Mayakovsky:

> There were two well-known phrases about that time.
> That it had become better and more fun to live, and
> that Mayakovsky was and remained the best and most
> talented poet of the epoch. . . . They started instituting
> Mayakovsky by force, like the potato during Catherine's
> reign. This was his second death. Of it he is innocent.[6]

Dire metaphors of second death aside, however, Stalin's edict was by no means unequivocally disastrous to Mayakovsky's legacy. The sinister addendum "Indifference to his memory and his works is a crime" instantly rescued the poet from oblivion and ensured that Mayakovsky would become one of the most written about of twentieth-century artists. Monuments were erected; squares and streets were renamed in his honor. The problem, of course, was that the only officially acceptable (and thus publishable) attitude toward Mayakovsky was one of blind adulation—an adulation based, again, not on literary criteria, but on a crudely politicized vision of the poet as Singer of the Socialist Revolution. Aspects of Mayakovsky's life and work that were incompatible with this simplified ideal—for example, his suicide, his affair with a Russian émigré in Paris, another affair in New York that resulted in an illegitimate child, and his close association with out-of-favor literary movements (including Futurism, Formalism, and others)—were downplayed or ignored altogether, with the result that Soviet criticism markedly favors Mayakovsky's postrevolutionary political verse. Not surprisingly, it is his prerevolutionary, primarily lyrical work that received the most attention and praise from his great contemporaries in poetry—including Pasternak and Marina Tsvetaeva—and from Western critics of the Cold War era. These two distinct and opposing views of the poet were for many years reluctant to combine or to learn anything significant from each other.

Even working within the confines of politically acceptable views on Mayakovsky, however, Soviet scholars accomplished a great deal. If the official conception of the poet was necessarily incomplete, it was nevertheless extraordinarily detailed. Vasily Katanian, a friend of the poet's, dedicated much of his life to the compilation and revision of a chronicle of Mayakovsky's life and work, with the result that we now have a practically day-by-day record of the poet's travels, publications, and public appearances.[7] Grigory Vinokur cataloged many of Mayakovsky's neologisms, unusual expressions, and linguistic innovations.[8] Among other Soviet-era scholars, Viktor Pertsov and Zinovy Paperny stand out as the most prolific and least crippled by ideological orthodoxy.[9] Using painstaking and thorough statistical analysis of Mayakovsky's entire oeuvre, Mikhail Gasparov left few stones unturned with regard to the poet's technique—his use of rhythm, rhyme, and unusual verse layouts.[10]

As perestroika brought about a gradual loosening of government censorship and an atmosphere of reevaluation and revision, a predictable critical backlash against Mayakovsky took shape. The generations of Soviet writers and critics born after Stalin's resolution, having been force-fed Mayakovsky as children and throughout their professional lives, wanted the opportunity to spit him out, as it were—to get him out of their systems. The best known of these revisionists was Yuri Karabchievsky, whose scathing *The Resurrection of Mayakovsky* (*Voskresenie Maiakovskogo*) was too outspoken to be published in the USSR, even in 1985, and was brought out by a Munich firm.[11] In fine polemical style, Karabchievsky seeks to invert nearly every accepted truth about the poet and to prove that Mayakovsky's generally acknowledged strengths—including the innovative language, poetic form, and metaphors discussed below—are in fact weaknesses. Karabchievsky's central thesis is that Mayakovsky is a poet obsessed with his own pain who celebrates murderous violence in his imagery as a way of getting back at the world that rejects him: "Two points, two poles, two morals: the greatest pain in the world when Mayakovsky has been hurt, and a physiological delight in violence when he is hurting someone else, avenging the wrong."[12] Karabchievsky uses this starting point to arrive at the conclusion that Mayakovsky welcomed the October Revolution not because of any ideological affinity with Marxism or love of humanity in the abstract, but because his prerevolutionary work made him uniquely prepared for the shameless vengeance the Bolsheviks would wreak on their enemies.[13]

Karabchievsky and other detractors of Mayakovsky, in turn, inspired interesting new apologias, which were no longer constrained by Soviet conceptions of the poet. Bronislav Gorb stands out among these new defenders of Mayakovsky, as his

Jester at the Throne of the Revolution (*Shut u trona revoliutsii*, 2001) offers a radical and comprehensive reinterpretation of Mayakovsky as poet and public figure.[14] Gorb attempts to provide a direct and definitive answer to a question that stumped the poet's friends and continues to perplex critics: simply put, when and to what extent was Mayakovsky joking, and when was he being serious? Gorb's answer, in short, is that he was always joking; Gorb contends that rather than serving the Bolshevik regime after the October Revolution, Mayakovsky immediately began to undermine it through satire, renewing age-old Russian traditions of foolery and buffoonery. Even in his most stridently pro-Soviet propaganda pieces, or especially in them, Gorb argues, Mayakovsky is in fact doing battle with the state, poking fun at its leaders and tenets with unthinkable sangfroid and disregard for the risks involved. It is an attractively bold and simply attractive argument, and one many fans of Mayakovsky's work no doubt wish were true, but Gorb's extreme formulation and his support of it are ultimately unconvincing. His readings demonstrate the dangers of using analysis of humor to support an essentially ideological approach to Mayakovsky: the passages Gorb identifies as undeniably ironic and satirical might just as easily be interpreted as sincere. His book is full of fresh, unconventional insights into Mayakovsky's work (a few are cited in my notes), but it suffers in the end because those insights are subordinated to a predetermined ideological orientation.

The general trend in post-Soviet Mayakovsky criticism has been away from such ideologically motivated studies, as critics move past the perceived need to justify or apologize for the poet and his unique legacy. The field has recovered from its genesis or re-genesis in Stalin's resolution, and scholars are approaching Mayakovsky in new and unexpected ways. Mikhail Weiskopf writes of Mayakovsky's religion—an oxymoronic formulation from the standpoint of the traditional view of the poet as a militant atheist—finding the basis for many of his thematic preoccupations in wide-ranging religious beliefs and practices, from ancient pagan rituals to Orthodox Christianity and shamanism.[15] Leonid Katsis's monumental *Vladimir Mayakovsky: A Poet in the Intellectual Context of the Epoch* (*Vladimir Maiakovskii: Poet v intellektual'nom kontekste epokhi*, 2004), as its subtitle implies, pays special attention to broad cultural contexts and the influence on Mayakovsky of his contemporaries and immediate predecessors in literature, art, music, and philosophy.[16] Katsis's conception of the poet flies in the face of the conventional understanding—reinforced deceptively by the poet himself—of Mayakovsky as an uneducated, street-smart rebel indifferent to such things as intellectual atmosphere. Furthermore, Katsis refuses to pick sides with regard to Mayakovsky's pre- and postrevolutionary work, and his argument that the latter can be understood in the context of Silver Age aesthetics and mysticism (rather than Soviet propaganda and bureaucracy) is compelling. Weiskopf, too, incorporates Mayakovsky's Soviet works impartially and seamlessly into his argument.

Thus, the major historical divide regarding Mayakovsky has been gradually overcome, but many questions remain, and the poet's legacy is still difficult to divorce from the ideological debates that framed it for so many years. This collection is designed with the goal of moving past those debates and reintroducing Mayakovsky to the anglophone world, focusing instead on his gifts and achievements as a poet.

Mayakovsky was a tireless innovator of language. Word creation and manipulation of grammar and morphology came naturally to him, even if they were never as conspicuous in his poetry as they were in that of his friends and fellow Cubo-Futurists Velimir Khlebnikov and Alexei Kruchenykh. Instead, Mayakovsky's work combines innovative expressions—language the Russian Formalists called *enstranged* and prized for its ability to prevent automatic recognition in the reader—with the all-too-clear, colloquial, and at times vulgar language of the·street.[17] The result is an idiom of indelible weirdness and frenetic energy.

Free movement between stylistic registers and authorial tones is a hallmark of Mayakovsky's verse, but many of his innovations celebrate freedom on an even more basic linguistic level. Particles and half-words that are no longer seen outside a single, tired stock phrase suddenly find themselves emancipated, combining with new words in new contexts.[18] Prepositions that would normally receive no semantic or metrical stress are made the focal point of an entire line, front and center under the spotlight of rhyme.[19] Nouns can change their grammatical gender, and intransitive verbs can become transitive at the drop of a hat. As Vinokur observed, many of Mayakovsky's linguistic departures from the norm serve to eliminate the boundary between animate and inanimate objects.[20] Possessive adjectives, to pick one tiny example, are formed from inanimate nouns, and as a result, a romance blossoms between the poet and a violin ("Violin and a Bit Nervously," 1914). The sun drops by for tea ("An Extraordinary Adventure . . . ," 1920). Empowered by Mayakovsky's language as much as by his ideology, cobblestones, trains, automobiles, skyscrapers, drugstores, and furniture join humans and beasts in the worldwide struggle of revolution ("150,000,000," 1919–1920). Airplanes bustle about like children ("The Flying Proletarian," 1925). People, animals, and things find themselves on one plane of universal familiarity, open to interactions and unexpected intimacies that typical language would either prevent altogether or hierarchize. Trite as it may sound, the world of Mayakovsky's language is strikingly egalitarian, and it is a world where anything can happen.

Mayakovsky also breathed new life into Russian poetic form. One thinks first of the unusual verse layouts—particularly the staircase (*lesenka*) pattern, which he began to use in 1923—that give much of his poetry its unmistakable, iconic look. But as Mikhail Gasparov and Gerald Janecek have demonstrated, Mayakovsky's layouts—both the staircase and the earlier column (*stolbik*)—were modeled to a large extent on experiments by the Symbolist poet Andrei Bely.[21] Thus, despite the fascinating mechanics of these systems of line division, and despite the profound effect they have on the experience of reading Mayakovsky's verse, they are not without precedent, and they are not his most radical contributions. Instead, it is his understanding of rhythm and rhyme that truly expanded the boundaries of the possible in Russian poetry. Though Mayakovsky composed, at one time or another, in nearly all the traditional syllabo-tonic meters—he typically used iambs for parodies, preferring trochees for lines he didn't wish to mark stylistically—he is best known for his accentual verse: lines with a set number of stresses, usually three or four, but few restrictions on the number of unstressed syllables falling between them. In Mayakovsky's verse, that number could reach five or more, which made his lines considerably freer and more unpredictable than the *dol'nik* (a verse line that allows for only one or two syllables between stresses) and other accentual verse traditions he inherited from his Symbolist forebears. He was also a master of sharp, staccato rhythms involving spondees and strings of semantically charged, monosyllabic words: he used such lines consistently and powerfully in militaristic poems such as "Our March" (1917) and the battle scenes in "150,000,000" and "The Flying Proletarian."

It is for his rhymes, however, that Mayakovsky is most often remembered. Early in his career, when his interest in verbal Cubism was strongest, he experimented with rhyming the end of one line with the beginning of the next ("Morning," 1912), and also used palindromic line fragments to memorable effect ("From Street to Street," 1913). Throughout his life, his notion of what constituted a rhyme would push against traditional definitions and limitations, broadening horizons and enriching what was already a rhyme-rich language. Many of Mayakovsky's rhymes are closer to what is called near-rhyme in English; assonance (the repetition of a stressed vowel sound) or even just consonance (a matching or near-matching of consonant sounds) were sometimes enough for him, but he was also adept at more flashy compound and multisyllabic rhymes.[22] He regularly used what he would come to call "whip rhymes"—rhymes in which a single-word cadence crushes or deflates multiple words at the end of its preceding rhyme-pair line.[23] Yuri Lotman found an interesting analogy for such rhymes, and one that could apply equally to many of Mayakovsky's signature poetic devices: they "create the effect of an enormous machine performing an insignificant task—bringing together distant concepts unexpectedly fails to give rise to new meaning, by virtue of the general insignificance of the content."[24] Lotman was referring to the outlandishly deflating rhymes in the 1923 poem "Schematic of Laughter," but one could certainly speak more generally of the poetic ends not justifying the means in Mayakovsky's work. Instead, the means—whether rhythm, rhyme, personification, or other—have a way of becoming ends in their own right. This is especially true of his metaphors.

Mayakovsky had a tendency to place himself in every landscape he described and every event or narrative he recounted; his poetic speaker is Vladimir Mayakovsky (often explicitly), and this lyrical stand-in is omnipresent in his work. He is larger than life, and often alienated, but thanks in part to the all-inclusive language described above, he is also open to all sorts of connections, mergers, and relationships; he understands the language of streets, squares, and buildings, and he converses with them, as well as with violins, horses, and the sun. Tsvetaeva noted this quality of his verse in her 1932 essay "Epic and Lyric in Contemporary Russia" ("Epos i lirika sovremennoi Rossii"):

> Mayakovsky is the I-in-everything. . . . Mayakovsky is the conversion of self into object, the dissolution of self in object. . . . Mayakovsky is faceless; he became the thing he was depicting. Mayakovsky as a noun is collective. . . . Mayakovsky represents the impossibility of *not* merging with one's surroundings.[25]

For Mayakovsky, then, a metaphor represents the invasion of the world into the poet's senses and the irresistible merger of those sensory impressions with his ego; it is no wonder that he loses control of his comparisons and other devices. In Mayakovsky's most characteristic metaphors, the tenor (the thing being described) is subordinate to the vehicle (the thing to which the tenor is compared), and the vehicle is often developed and expanded to the extent that it takes over the poem. In "The Cloud in Pants" (1914–1915), he riffs on the old cliché of a "heart on fire" with love:

> The people catch a whiff—
> it smells like burnt flesh!
> They've gathered some men.
> All shiny!
> In helmets!
> But hey, no boots allowed!
> Inform the firemen:
> you climb up to a burning heart with caresses.[26]

In the later "I Love" (1922), the slightly different but equally tired metaphor of a "heavy heart" receives similar treatment:

> Beneath the weight
> my legs

took wobbly steps—
as you know,
I'm
pretty well built—
but even so,
I trailed along like my heart's appendage,
my broad shoulders bent out of shape.[27]

Such metaphors are commonly described as *realized,* and Maya-kovsky was a compulsive realizer of metaphors and other poetic devices. In "Jubilee," his apostrophe to the Moscow Pushkin monument, which would traditionally be a vertical, hierarchical form of communication, is instantly brought down to the horizontal and familiar level as the speaker drags the statue down from its pedestal (realizing the metaphor) and takes it on a walking tour of the city. Mayakovsky's understanding of figurative language was consistently and often disarmingly literal.

When speaking of Mayakovsky's themes and poetic poses (the attitudes and orientations of his lyrical persona), it is easy to get lost in contradictions and paradoxes, and it is important not to let these calcify into false dichotomies. Like Walt Whit-man, to whom he has been compared, Mayakovsky contained multitudes.[28] He is one of the twentieth century's quintessential poets of bombastic self-aggrandizement, even megalomania, and yet he dreamed constantly—and wrote frequently—about self-annihilation, ultimately committing suicide. His lyrical alter ego alternates between spitting in the public's face and begging for attention and understanding, between wreaking bloody revenge on his enemies and saving the entire world through his enormous capacity for suffering. He is presented as the most lonely, misunderstood hero in the world, and yet also a successful ringleader and member of the victorious col-lective. All these themes and attitudes, again, can be traced through the early and late poetry, from the 1913 cycle "Me" to the 1930 cri de coeur "At the Top of My Voice." Their at times overwhelming melodrama, however, is also tempered throughout his oeuvre with whimsy—with buoyantly inventive images that lighten the overall mood and suggest that Mayakovsky's lyrical hero is more self-aware and ironic than he seems. He concludes the fiery urban apocalypse of the 1914 poem "But Be That as It May" with the marvelous image of God running around heaven with Mayakovsky's poems tucked in his armpit, reading them to his acquaintances (1:62). He turns from the epic air battle depicted in the first section of "The Flying Proletarian" to an absurd utopia reminiscent of *The Jetsons,* realizing, as it were, the metaphor "flight of fancy."

A final and critically important theme running through Mayakovsky's body of work is the poet's tooth-and-nail struggle against convention, bourgeois taste, and the monotonous, daily capitulations of labor and life, both public and private (all these opponents are summed up neatly in the Russian word *byt*). Though he saw the revolutions of 1917 as an important milestone in that personal struggle, they by no means represented victory, and for Mayakovsky, the battle raged on. Indeed, one could make the case—and Mayakovsky certainly tried—that he was a fighter before he ever was a poet. He writes in "I Myself" of the wooden sword he made as a boy to imitate Don Quixote (a telling role model), and of fighting with other children down by the Rioni River in Kutaisi, Georgia.[29] He joined the Bolshevik faction of the Russian Social-Democratic Labor Party in 1908, at the age of fourteen, and was arrested three times as an adolescent for revolutionary activities, eventually spending eleven months in a Moscow prison. He remained a fighter to the end, even as he succumbed: in an addendum to his suicide note, he chided himself for not finishing an argument with an associate ("we should have fought it out").[30]

Mayakovsky's fighting spirit was shaped in no small part by the literary and artistic milieu in which he came of age, and by his peers and early mentors. From his very first publications and throughout his early career, he was a member of the Hylaea group of Moscow Cubo-Futurists. Futurism, which began in Italy as a movement in the avant-garde visual arts, had made its way to Russia, where it became a group of splinter cells loosely bound by a few common concerns: keen interest in new forms and modes of artistic expression, antipathy toward classicism and old art, and often an interest in technology, speed, and anti-aesthetic urban imagery.[31] The ties to the visual arts remained strong in Russian Futurism; both Mayakovsky and his friend and mentor David Burliuk were poets and painters, and the *cubo* in Cubo-Futurism attested to the group's interest in Cubist painting. Mayakovsky's Futurist beginnings instilled in him the idea that art was a constant struggle: a struggle for the new and against the old. From the moment Mayakovsky began writing verse, he was belting it out on stage to hostile audiences, shouting to drown out jeers and laughter, and railing against the classics of art and literature in heated public debates. He toured Russia with his Cubo-Futurist cohorts in 1913 and 1914, and they were received all over the country as a cross between dangerous rabble-rousers and a circus troupe. The Futurists seemed almost to publish more manifestos than they did poetry, and there was much infighting between the various Futurist groups throughout the 1910s.[32]

In a sense, these battles—and Mayakovsky's central part in them—continued right on through the revolutions of 1917 and into early Soviet literary life. Though Futurism as such became less relevant after the Civil War, there were numerous groups jockeying for leadership in the new hierarchy of Soviet literature in the 1920s. Mayakovsky was associated in the mid-1920s with Lef (the Left Front of the Arts), a group he claimed represented the continuation of Futurism (see the section on Lef in "I Myself"), though the connections are not obvious. Lef and especially New Lef, the group's reincarnation in 1927, favored journalism, slogans, and other genres of what they called "the literature of fact"; they were explicitly against fiction and imaginative writing. The violence Mayakovsky would wreak against his own poetic style in order to conform to this increasingly extreme theoretical stance was one of his last battles as a writer. His life's work is imbued with a powerful sense of these many struggles, and it is intentional on Mayakovsky's part, inevitable, and appropriate that his legacy has inspired such impassioned debate. The debate should be grounded, however, in the words he fought so hard to create, declaim, publish, and defend. He is a poet who demands to be heard, to be wrestled with, to be poked and prodded, and his continuing relevance depends on this immediacy and spirit of direct engagement. This collection intends to bring Mayakovsky back into close range for new generations of anglophone sparring partners.

Notes

1. V. V. Maiakovskii, *Polnoe sobranie sochinenii v trinadtsati tomakh* (Moscow: Gosudarstvennoe izdatel'stvo khudozhestvennoi literatury, 1955–61), 6:49. Further references to Mayakovsky's works are to this edition and are identified by volume and page number only. Single slashes (/) indicate a step break within Mayakovsky's staircase verse, and double slashes (//) indicate the end of an entire staircase line. Unless otherwise noted, translations from the Russian are mine throughout.

2. R. Jakobson, "On a Generation That Squandered Its Poets," in *Language in Literature,* ed. Krystyna Pomorska and Stephen Rudy, trans. Edward J. Brown (Cambridge, Mass.: Harvard University Press, 1987), 275–76. Jakobson's is one of the most perceptive and important essays ever written on Mayakovsky.

3. For a facsimile, typescript, and other information on Lily Brik's letter and Stalin's resolution, see S. E. Strizhneva, ed., *"V tom, chto umiraiu, ne vinite nikogo"? Sledstvennoe delo V. V. Maiakovskogo* (Moscow: Ellis Lak 2000, 2005), 317–24.

4. The initiative to write the letter was not Brik's; it was the product of a group meeting in the Kremlin apartment of Yakov Agranov (ibid., 324). Still, by agreeing to be the sole signer of the letter, Brik took upon herself the considerable risk involved in appealing directly to Stalin.

5. "Jubilee" (6:54).

6. From the memoir *Liudi i polozheniia* (1956–57). B. Pasternak, *Sobranie sochinenii v piati tomakh* (Moscow: Khudozhestvennaia literatura, 1991), 4:338.

7. V. A. Katanian, *Maiakovskii: Khronika zhizni i deiatel'nosti*, 5th ed. (Moscow: Sovetskii pisatel', 1985).

8. G. Vinokur, *Maiakovskii novator iazyka* (Moscow: Sovetskii pisatel', 1943).

9. V. Pertsov, *Maiakovskii: Zhizn' i tvorchestvo*, 3 vols. (Moscow: Nauka, 1969–72); Z. Papernyi, *Poeticheskii obraz u Maiakovskogo* (Moscow: Izdatel'stvo Akademii nauk SSSR, 1961).

10. M. Gasparov's prolific writings on the poet are spread across many articles and books, but perhaps most central is the section on Mayakovsky in *Sovremennyi russkii stikh: Metrika i ritmika* (Moscow: Nauka, 1974). A more general overview of Mayakovsky's poetics in its historical context is provided in *Ocherk istorii russkogo stikha* (Moscow: Fortuna, 2002).

11. Iu. A. Karabchievskii, *Voskresenie Maiakovskogo: Filologicheskii roman. Esse* (1985; Moscow: Russkie slovari, 2000), 4.

12. Ibid., 15.

13. Ibid., 18.

14. B. Gorb, *Shut u trona revoliutsii: Vnutrennii siuzhet tvorchestva i zhizni poeta i aktera Serebrianogo veka Vladimira Maiakovskogo* (Moscow: Uliss-Media, 2001).

15. M. Vaiskopf, *Vo ves' logos: Religiia Maiakovskogo* (Moscow: Salamandra, 1997).

16. L. F. Katsis, *Vladimir Maiakovskii: Poet v intellektual'nom kontekste epokhi*, 2nd ed. (Moscow: Rossiiskii gosudarstvennyi gumanitarnyi universitet, 2004).

17. "Enstrangement" is Benjamin Sher's translation of Viktor Shklovsky's term *ostranenie* (making strange). V. B. Shklovsky, *Theory of Prose*, trans. B. Sher (Normal, Ill.: Dalkey Archive Press, 1990), 6–9.

18. Examples include Mayakovsky's combination of «в оба» (in both), typically seen only in the expression «смотреть в оба» (to keep both eyes peeled), with the verb «светить» (to shine) in the 1920 poem "An Extraordinary Adventure . . ." (2:37); and his liberation of the intensifying adverb «ревмя» from the phrase «ревмя реветь» (to wail or

bellow) to combine with the verb «выть» (to howl) in the 1923 poem "Schematic of Laughter" (5:38).

19. See, for example, the following passage from "Jubilee": «...но смотрите— / из // выплывают / Red и White Star'ы // с ворохом / разнообразных виз» ("... but look— / from // Red and White Stars / are weighing anchor // in a flurry / of assorted visas," 6:49, emphasis added).

20. Vinokur, *Maiakovskii novatov iazyka*, 45.

21. Gasparov, *Sovremennyi russkii stikh*, 436–37; G. Janecek, *The Look of Russian Literature: Avant-Garde Visual Experiments, 1900–1930* (Princeton, N.J.: Princeton University Press, 1984), 219–23.

22. Here are just a few of Mayakovsky's tenuous rhymes: скомкан / окон ("Night," 1:33); самого / самовар ("An Extraordinary Adventure . . . ," 2:36–37); хоть / начхать, паровоз / про вас, лента / Лермонтов (all from "Tamara and the Demon," 6:76); сломал / слова ("Conversation with a Taxman About Poetry," 7:120).

23. Mayakovsky referred to "the craftsmanship of whip rhymes" (выделк[а] хлыстов-рифм) in the foreword to his collection of satirical verse *Mayakovsky Smiles, Mayakovsky Laughs, Mayakovsky Mocks* (*Maiakovskii ulybaetsia, Maiakovskii smeetsia, Maiakovskii izdevaetsia*, 12:52). He was describing the rhymes in his 1923 poem "Schematic of Laughter," which include: знал о ком / молоком, дрожь нам / железнодорожным, карьер с Оки / курьерский, сто свистков ревмя / вовремя, звёзды дым / воздадим, etc. (5:38).

24. Iu. Lotman, *O poetakh i poezii* (St. Petersburg: Iskusstvo–SPb, 2001), 237.

25. M. Tsvetaeva, *Sobranie sochinenii v semi tomakh* (Moscow: Ellis Lak, 1994), 5:380–81. Tsvetaeva's essay contrasts Mayakovsky with Pasternak; in the omitted portions of this passage, she describes Pasternak as Mayakovsky's opposite.

26. 1:180.

27. 4:90.

28. Kornei Chukovsky, an early translator of Whitman into Russian and a friend of Mayakovsky's, thought much of the connection between the two poets. Western critics including Clare Cavanagh and Dale Peterson have also written of it: C. Cavanagh, "Whitman, Mayakovsky, and the Body Politic," in *Rereading Russian Poetry*, ed. Stephanie Sandler (New Haven, Conn.: Yale University Press, 1999); D. Peterson, "Mayakovsky and Whitman: The Icon and the Mosaic," *Slavic Review* 28, no. 3 (1969): 416–25.

29. 1:12–13.

30. For a facsimile of the suicide note, see Strizhneva, ed., *Sledstvennoe delo*, 39–45.

31. Vladimir Markov's *Russian Futurism: A History* (Washington, D.C.: New Academia, 2006), first published in 1968, is still an excellent source of information on the convoluted and fascinating history of the movement.

32. A fine collection of primary sources on Russian Futurism is A. Lawton and H. Eagle, eds., *Words in Revolution: Russian Futurist Manifestoes 1912–1928* (Washington, D.C.: New Academia, 2005).

Translating Mayakovsky is a daunting task. The traditional impossibility of verse translation—maintaining poetic form and semantic content—is compounded in his case by Mayakovsky's penchant for word creation and highly unusual, at times ambiguous, grammar. Furthermore, form—which comprises rhythm, rhyme, all sorts of sound-play, and other effects that rely on the phonetic or graphic makeup of words in Russian—is almost always a bearer of meaning, and it is often so central to Mayakovsky's work that to throw it out entirely would render a poem meaningless. There is also the challenge of conveying Mayakovsky's frequent changes in tone and stylistic register: from jeering to pleading, from vulgarity to eloquence (or mock eloquence), from bathos to pathos and back again. My overall goal as a translator is to convey with maximum precision the meaning of Mayakovsky's words while remaining sensitive to these shifts in style and attitude. If Mayakovsky conspicuously uses a neologism or an unusual expression, I try to find an approximate equivalent in English (examples include "goldilobe" and "lume" from the 1920 poem "An Extraordinary Adventure . . ."), explaining my choice in a note if necessary. Of course, there could be wide disagreement as to what constitutes a conspicuous neologism, and in any case, some of Mayakovsky's innovative uses of language inevitably slip through the cracks of both my translations and notes.

My position with regard to rhythm and rhyme is more complicated. I sacrificed these to semantic fidelity in the vast majority of cases, drawing attention in notes to effects that are particularly important or unusual in the original. I did, however, preserve a few rhymes and rhythms, whenever I deemed it possible to do so without significant damage to Mayakovsky's meaning. Looking back to the three widely acknowledged strengths of Mayakovsky's poetry discussed in the introduction—powerful metaphors, innovative language, and groundbreaking poetic form—my hope is that my translations alone preserve much of the first two, and that the combination of my translations and notes will give the reader some understanding of the third.

Selecting poems for this volume was far less difficult than translating them: with few exceptions, I went with the poems I find most interesting. One of my goals was to present in their entirety works that are familiar to Western readers, if at all, only in excerpts: among these are the autobiography "I Myself" and the long political poems "150,000,000" and "The Flying Proletarian." The result is a collection that favors, at least in terms of space, Mayakovsky's long poems (called *poemy* in Russian) over other genres. It is in these long poems that Mayakovsky's lyricism and idiosyncratic brand of propaganda find their fullest and most characteristic expression, and his reputation as a poet rests disproportionately on them. As for the shorter poems I chose to include, I tried to pick works that would be simultaneously less familiar and more accessible—with proper commentary—to Western readers (e.g., "Jubilee" and "Conversation with a Taxman About Poetry").

My notes are intended to be informative rather than interpretive. Mayakovsky's autobiography and poetry are filled with references to current events, half-forgotten Soviet agencies and organizations, and his contemporaries and predecessors in culture and politics. Many of these are completely unknown to nonspecialists, so informational notes are frequently necessary to make Mayakovsky accessible to the modern reader. The notes, comprising introductory remarks for each poem (which are designed to provide a way into the text for readers less familiar with Mayakovsky and his era) and explanations of various key words and passages, are grouped in a section at the end of the book, to make them less intrusive and to enable a pure reading of the poems. Most critical apparatuses rely on a combination of reference works and previous commentaries, and mine is no different. I am particularly indebted to the commentary provided in the standard edition of Mayakovsky's works—the thirteen-volume Soviet Academy of Sciences edition published from 1955 to 1961—and to Edward J. Brown's critical biography *Mayakovsky: A Poet in the Revolution* (1973), still one of the best English-language books on Mayakovsky. The Academy edition is also my source for the original texts of his works, and it is available in full online, free of charge, at the following address: http://www.feb-web.ru/feb/mayakovsky/default.asp.*

*The Fundamental Electronic Library (http://www.feb-web.ru/) is an online repository of full-text materials on Russian literature and folklore.

Selected Poems

I Myself

The Theme

I'm a poet. That's what makes me interesting. So that's what I'm writing about. As for all the other stuff—only if it's settled down in words.

Memory

Burliuk used to say "Mayakovsky's got a memory like a road in Poltava—everyone leaves a galosh stuck in the mud." But I can't keep track of faces or dates. I only remember that in the year 1100, some kind of "nobbles" moved from one place to another. I don't remember the details, but I guess it must have been a pretty serious affair. Anyway, it's just petty to memorize things like "This was written on May 2 in Pavlovsk, by the fountains." And so I swim freely through my chronology.

The Main Thing

Born July 7, 1894 (or '93—Father's service record and Mama disagree on the subject; in any case, no earlier). Hometown: Bagdadi, a village in the Kutaisi province of Georgia.

Family Members

Father: Vladimir Konstantinovich (a Bagdadi forest warden), died in 1906. Mama: Alexandra Alexeyevna. Sisters: a) Lyuda, b) Olya. There would appear to be no other Mayakovskys.

First Memory

Pictorial. Place unknown. Winter. Father subscribed to the magazine *Homeland*. *Homeland* had a humor supplement. Everyone was talking about the funnies and waiting. Father was pacing and singing his usual "alon zanfan de la two three four." *Homeland* came. I opened it and immediately (a picture) bawled out: "How funny! The man and the lady are kissing." Everyone laughed. Later, when the supplement came and it was really time to laugh, it became clear—earlier they had only been laughing at me. And so our concepts of pictures and humor diverged.

Second Memory

Poetic. Summer. Tons of visitors. A tall, handsome student, Boris Glushkovsky. He could draw. Had an enormous leather sketchbook. Beautiful paper. On one page there was a tall man with no pants on (or maybe with very tight ones). His name was "You-jean-on-eggin." Both Boris and the man in the drawing were tall. It was obvious. Boris must be this You-jean-on-eggin character. I thought that way for about three years.

Third Memory

Practical. Nighttime. Mama and Papa whispering endlessly behind the wall. About a piano. I couldn't sleep all night. One sentence kept irritating me. In the morning I came running: "Papa, what's an installment plan?" Got a kick out of the explanation.

Bad Habits

Summer. Staggering quantities of guests. The name days piled up. Father bragged about my memory. I was forced to memorize poetry for all the name days. I remember, for Papa's name day, it was:

> Once upon a time, before a throng
> Of kindred mountains . . .

"Kindred" and "precipices" bothered me. Who they were, I didn't know, and I never seemed to come across them in life. Later I learned that these were poeticisms and began quietly to hate them.

Romantic Roots

The first house I remember clearly. Two floors. The top one was ours. Below was a little winery. Once a year there were carts of grapes. They crushed them. I ate. They drank. This was all on the territory of an ancient Georgian stronghold near Bagdadi. The fortress was enclosed by a rectangular rampart. Turrets at the corners for cannons. Gun-slots in the walls. Past the ramparts were moats. Past the moats, forests and jackals. Above the forests, mountains. I grew up. Ran to the top of the highest one. The mountains were lower to the north. To the north there was a gap. The Russia of my dreams was out there. I was unbelievably drawn to it.

Extraordinary

About seven years old. Father started taking me with him on his forestry inspections. A mountain pass. Night. Fog all around.

Couldn't even see my father in front of me. He must have gotten a dog rose branch caught on his sleeve. The branch with its thorns swung right into my face. Squealing a bit, I pulled out the prickles. Then the fog and the pain immediately disappeared. The parting fog beneath my feet was suddenly brighter than the sky. It was electricity. Prince Nakashidze's rivet factory. Once I saw electricity, I completely lost interest in nature. An unimproved thing.

Studies

At first I was taught by Mama and various female cousins. Arithmetic seemed unrealistic. You had to count the apples and pears given out to little boys. Whereas I always gave and received without counting. In the Caucasus there was as much fruit as you could eat. I enjoyed learning to read.

First Book

Something like *The Chicken Farmer Agafia*. A few more like that and I would have quit reading altogether. Fortunately, my second was *Don Quixote*. Now there's a book! Made a wooden sword and armor, tilted at everything I could find.

Exam

We moved. From Bagdadi to Kutaisi. Entrance exam for the gymnasium. I passed. They asked about the anchor (on my sleeve)—*that* I knew. But a priest asked what an *oko* was. I answered: "three pounds" (that's what it means in Georgian). The courteous examiners explained to me that *oko* is the Old

Church Slavonic for "eye." Almost failed because of that. I immediately began hating everything old, everything church, and everything Slavonic. It could be that my Futurism, atheism, and internationalism all stem from this incident.

Gymnasium

Kindergarten, first, and second grade. First in my class. All A's. Reading Jules Verne. Science fiction in general. Some guy with a beard discovered in me the makings of an artist. Taught me for free.

War with Japan

The number of newspapers and magazines around the house increased. *The Russian Bulletin, The Russian Word, Russian Riches,* and others. I read them all. Was unaccountably worked up. Loved all the postcards of battleships. Copied them, redrew them bigger. The word "proclamation" appeared. Georgians hung proclamations. Cossacks hung Georgians. My friends were Georgians. I started to hate Cossacks.

Underground Literature

My sister arrived from Moscow. Gushing. Gave me leaflets on the sly. I liked them: it was all so risky. I remember them even now. The first:

> Snap out of it, comrade; snap out of it, brother,
> throw down your rifle right now.

And another one, one that ended:

> . . . otherwise, the path leads elsewhere—
> to the Germans, with your son, wife, and mommy . . .

(about the tsar).

It was the revolution. It was in verse. Poetry and the revolution somehow joined together in my mind.

1905

In no mood for studying. Started getting C's. Made it to fourth grade only because I got hit in the head with a rock (fighting down by the Rioni)—they took pity on me at the exam retake. The revolution began for me as follows: my comrade Isidor, a priest's cook, jumped up on the stove barefoot with joy—General Alikhanov had been killed. The repressor of Georgia. Protests and rallies started. I went to them. It was good. Took it all in vividly: the anarchists in black, SRs in red, SDs in blue, and federalists in all the other colors.

Socialism

Speeches, newspapers. All filled with unfamiliar concepts and words. I needed explanations, needed to find them myself. Little white booklets in the windows. The Stormy Petrel. All about the same thing. Bought them all. Woke up at six in the morning. Read insatiably. First: *Down with the Social-Democrats.* Next: *Economic Debates.* All my life I've been struck by socialists' ability to confuse facts, to systematize the world. *What to Read?* by Rubakin, I think. I read and reread what was recommended to me. Didn't understand a lot of it. Asked about it. Ended up being led to a Marxist circle. Hit upon "The Erfurt Program."

In the middle. About the lumpen proletariat. Started consid-
ering myself a Social Democrat: stole my father's Berdan rifles
and brought them to the SD committee.

I liked Lassalle as a figure. Probably because he didn't have
a beard. He looked young. I confused Lassalle with Demos-
thenes. Went down to the Rioni. Practiced giving speeches
with rocks in my mouth.

Reaction

The way I see it, it all started with the following: at a public
demonstration in memory of Bauman, there was a panic, and I
got hit in the head by an enormous drum (I had fallen down).
I got scared because I thought the popping sound had come
from me.

1906

Father died. Pricked his finger sewing papers together. Blood
poisoning. To this day I can't stand needles. Our days of pros-
perity were over. After Father's funeral we were left with three
rubles. Instinctively, feverishly, we sold all our tables and chairs.
Set off for Moscow. Why? We didn't even know anyone there.

The Road

Baku was the best part. Towers, cisterns, the best smells—
petroleum, and then the steppe. Even the desert.

Moscow

Stopped in Razumovskoe. Friends of my sister's, the Plotnikovs. In the morning we took a train to Moscow. Got an apartment on Bronnaya.

Life in Moscow

Not enough to eat. A pension of ten rubles a month. My sisters and I were in school. Mama had to rent out rooms and cook dinners. The rooms were crap. The students who stayed with us were poor. Socialists. I remember—the first "Bolshevik" I ever saw was Vasya Kandelaki.

Something Pleasant

Was sent out to get kerosene. Given five rubles. At the store they gave me fourteen rubles and 50 kopecks' change—ten rubles pure profit. Conscience got the better of me. Walked around the store a couple times ("Erfurt" gnawing away at me). Quietly asked the salesman, "Who made the mistake, the owner or the worker?" "The owner!" Bought and ate four fruit-cakes. Spent the rest on a boat ride at the Patriarch's Ponds. To this day I can't stand the sight of fruitcake.

Work

The family had no money. We had to draw and do wood-burning. I especially remember the Easter eggs. Round, spinning and creaking like doors. I sold the eggs to a homemade crafts store on Neglinnaya. Ten to fifteen kopecks apiece. To this day I have endless contempt for Bohms, the Russian style, and all handicrafts.

Gymnasium

Transferred to the fourth grade class at Gymnasium No. 5. D's and the occasional C for variety. *Anti-Dühring* hidden under my desk.

Reading

Absolutely no respect for literature. Preferred philosophy. Hegel. Natural science. But mainly Marxism. No work of art could have interested me more than Marx's "Preface." There was a stream of underground publications from the student lodgers' rooms. *Street-Fighting Tactics,* etc. I clearly remember a little book bound in dark blue, Lenin's *Two Tactics.* I liked that the pages were cut right up to the edge of the letters. To make it easier to shove into a pocket and pass around illegally. The aesthetics of maximal economy.

First Quasi-Poem

Gymnasium No. 3 published a little underground journal, *The Impulse.* It made me mad. Other people are writing, and I can't?! Started scribbling. What came out was incredibly revolutionary and just as incredibly hideous. Like Kirillov is now. Can't remember a single line. Wrote another poem. This one came out lyrical. Not considering such a state of mind to be compatible with my "socialist dignity," I quit writing altogether.

The Party

1908. Joined the RSDLP (Bolsheviks). Was tested in the area of trade/industry. Passed. Became a propagandist. Went to the bakers first, then the cobblers, and finally the printers. At the citywide conference I was elected to the Moscow Committee. Lomov, Povolzhets, Smidovich, and others were there. Called myself Comrade Konstantin. Didn't get a chance to work there, though—I got caught.

Arrest

Walked into an ambush in Gruziny on March 29, 1908. Our illegal printing press. I ate an address book. A hardcover. Taken to Presnenskaya Station. The secret police. Then Sushchevskaya Station. Inspector Voltanovsky (who obviously considered himself very clever) made me take dictation (I was accused of writing proclamations). I hopelessly garbled the dictation. Wrote "soshul-dimo-kratic." Seems to have worked. They let me out on bail. While at the station, I read through *Sanin* and was puzzled. For some reason there was a copy at every precinct. The cops must have considered it edifying.

Got out. Worked for the party for another year. Then another short prison term. They found a revolver on me. A friend of my father's, named Makhmudbekov, who happened to be arrested in the same ambush, said the revolver was his, and they let me go. At the time he was an assistant to the chief of the Kresty prison.

Third Arrest

The people living with us—Koridze (code name Morchadze), Gerulaitis, and others—were tunneling under the Taganka. To free some female political prisoners. We were able to arrange a jailbreak from the Novinskaya prison. I got caught. Wouldn't sit still. Kept brawling. They transferred me from precinct to precinct—Basmannaya, Meshchanskaya, Myasnitskaya, etc.—and finally—Butyrki. Solitary confinement cell #103.

Eleven Months in Butyrki

A very important time for me. After three years of theory and practice, I plunged into literature.

Read all the latest stuff. The Symbolists—Bely, Balmont. I was floored by the formal innovation. But it was alien to me. The themes and images weren't from my life. I tried to write just as well, but about other things. As it turned out, to write *the same about other things* was impossible. It came out stilted and snivelutionary. Something like:

> The forests were draped in gold and purple;
> On the domes of cathedrals sunlight played.
> I waited, but days became lost in months,
> Hundreds of wearisome days.

I filled a whole notebook with this stuff. My thanks to the guards—they confiscated it from me when I left. Otherwise I might have published it!

When I was done with modernity, I pounced on the classics. Byron, Shakespeare, Tolstoy. My last book was *Anna Karenina*. Didn't finish it. Was summoned away at night with all my things. To this day I don't know how it turned out for them, the Karenins.

They let me out. I was supposed to be exiled for three years to Turukhansk (the secret police had decreed it). Makhmud-bekov got me out of it by petitioning Kurlov.

During my incarceration I was tried in connection with my first arrest—they found me guilty, but I was a minor. So I was released on parental recognizance, and under police observation.

The So-Called Dilemma

I came out of prison agitated. Those I had read were the so-called greats. But how easy it would be to write better! I already had the right attitude toward the world. All I needed was experience in the arts. Where could I get it? I was an ignoramus. I needed some serious schooling. But by this time I had been kicked out of the gymnasium, and even out of the Stroganoff school. To keep working for the party, I would have had to go underground. As I saw it, I couldn't get an education underground. My only prospects there were to spend my life writing fliers, laying out ideas from other people's books—the right books, but not mine. If you held me upside down and shook out everything I had read, what would remain? The Marxist method. But hadn't that weapon fallen into childish hands? It's easy to handle if you're only dealing with like-minded people. But what would happen when I encountered the enemy? After all, I couldn't really write any better than Bely. He went on cheerily in his vein—"flung a pineapple into the heavens"—whereas I just whimpered in mine—"hundreds of wearisome days." Other party members had it better than I did. They had even had some university. (I respected higher education at the time—I didn't know what it was yet!)

What did I have to pit against the old aesthetic that was weighing me down? Wasn't the revolution sure to demand some serious schooling of me? I went to see Medvedev, at that time still one of my party comrades. Said I wanted to make socialist art. Seryozha got a good laugh out of that and said I didn't have the guts.

As it turns out, I think he may have underestimated my guts.

I stopped working for the party. I settled down and hit the books.

The Beginnings of Mastery

Thought to myself: I can't write poetry. My attempts had been pitiful. So I took up painting instead. Studied under Zhukovsky. Together with some nice little ladies, helped to paint nice little silver tea sets. Realized after a year that I was only learning how to do fancy needlework. Left to study under Kelin. A realist. A good artist. My best teacher. Firm. Mercurial.

What I needed was mastery: Holbein. The enemy of all things cute.

One poet I respected was Sasha Chorny. I enjoyed his anti-aestheticism.

Last School

Worked on heads for a year. Enrolled in the School of Painting, Sculpture, and Architecture: the only place where they'd accept you without any certificate of trustworthiness. Worked hard.

Was surprised to find out: the imitators were pampered while the independent ones were persecuted. Larionov, Mashkov. Revinstinct made me side with the ones who got expelled.

David Burliuk

Burliuk showed up at the school. Had an insolent look about him. Wore a lorgnette. And a frock coat. Walked around humming. I started trying to pick a fight. It almost came to blows.

In the Smoking Room

The Noble Assembly Hall. A concert. Rachmaninoff. *Isle of the Dead.* I had to escape the unbearable, melodized boredom. A minute later, Burliuk joined me. We laughed at each other. Went out for a walk together.

A Most Memorable Night

A conversation. We proceeded from boredom with Rachmaninoff to boredom with school, from boredom with school—to boredom with all classicism. David had the anger of a master who had left his contemporaries behind, and I had the pathos of a socialist who knew the inevitability of the downfall of the old. Russian Futurism was born.

The Next Night

During the day, a poem came out of me. Or rather, pieces of a poem. Bad ones. Unpublished. Night came. Sretensky Boulevard. I read the lines to Burliuk. Said a friend of a friend had written them. David stopped. Looked me up and down. Then bellowed: "You wrote that yourself! And you, why, you're a brilliant poet!" The use of such a grandiose and undeserved epithet in reference to me made me happy. I crossed over to poetry for good. That evening, completely unexpectedly, I became a poet.

Burliuk's Antics

The next morning Burliuk, introducing me to someone, boomed out: "You don't know each other? My brilliant friend. The famous poet Mayakovsky." I elbowed him. But Burliuk was adamant. Even growled at me as he walked away: "Now write. Otherwise you'll put me in a most idiotic position."

And So Every Day

I had to write. And write I did, my first poem (first professional, published poem)—"The crimson and white"—and others.

The Wonderful Burliuk

I think of David with constant affection. A wonderful friend. My true teacher. Burliuk made me a poet. Read me Frenchmen and Germans. Shoved books at me. Paced and talked incessantly. Wouldn't let me out of his sight. Gave me fifty kopecks every day. So I could write without going hungry.

Took me to his place at Novaya Mayachka for Christmas. I brought "Port" and other poems.

The Slap

We returned from Mayachka. Our views may have been vague, but our temperaments were razor-sharp. Khlebnikov was in Moscow. His quiet genius was at that time completely drowned out for me by David's seething bustle. Kruchenykh too was fluttering about, that Futurist Jesuit of words.

After a few nights of writing we birthed a joint manifesto. David gathered everything together and copied it out, the two of us gave it a name and published *A Slap in the Face to Public Taste*.

The Natives Get Restless

The Jack of Diamonds exhibits. Public debates. Furious speeches from David and me. The newspapers started to be filled with Futurism. The tone wasn't particularly polite. I, for example, was simply called a "son of a bitch."

The Yellow Blouse

I never had any suits. I had two blouses, both hideously vile in appearance. The tried-and-true method was to adorn oneself with a necktie. But I had no money. I got a big piece of yellow cloth from my sister. Tied it round. Caused a furor. Evidently the most noticeable and beautiful thing about a man was his tie. Hence, obviously, if you enlarged the tie, you'd enlarge the furor. Since there were limits to the size of a tie, I tried something tricky, instead: I made my tie into a shirt and my shirt into a tie.

The impression was irresistible.

Of Course

The artistic High Command bared its teeth. Prince Lvov. Principal of the school. Suggested we quit our criticism and agitation. We refused.

A council of "artists" expelled us from the school.

A Fun Year

We traveled across Russia. Evening programs. Lectures. Regional governors were on the alert. In Nikolaevo they suggested we say nothing about the authorities or Pushkin. We were often cut off by the police in the middle of a presentation. Vasya Kamensky joined our merry band. The oldest Futurist.

For me these years were spent working on form, mastering the word.

Publishers wouldn't touch us. The capitalist nose sensed dynamiters in us. No one bought a single line from me.

We returned to Moscow, where I lived mostly out on the streets.

This period came to a close with my tragedy *Vladimir Mayakovsky*. We staged it in Petersburg. Luna Park. They booed holes in it.

Early 1914

I could feel my mastery. I was ready to take charge of a theme. For real. But what theme? A revolutionary one. Thought about "The Cloud in Pants."

War

Welcomed it with great anxiety. At first just from the stand-point of décor and bluster. Did posters on commission—quite militaristic, of course. Later in verse. "War Is Declared."

August

The first battle. Faced with the horror of war. The war was disgusting. The home front, even worse. To tell people about war you have to see it for yourself. I went to enlist as a volunteer. They wouldn't let me. I was too unreliable.

Even Colonel Model got one thing right.

Winter

Revulsion and hatred for the war. "Ach, shut their eyes, shut the newspapers' eyes" and other poems.

Lost all interest in art.

May

Won sixty-five rubles. Took a trip to Finland. Kuokkala.

Kuokkala

The seven-acquaintance rotation (seven-field)—I made seven friends to eat dinner with. On Sunday it was Chukovsky, on Monday, Yevreinov, and so on. Thursday was the worst—I had to eat Repin's grass. For a seven-foot-tall Futurist, that's no way to live.

In the evening I walked along the beach. Worked on "The Cloud."

An awareness of imminent revolution grew stronger.

Went to Mustamiaki. To see Maxim Gorky. Read him parts of "The Cloud." Gorky was moved, cried all over my vest. My verse had unsettled him. I started to get cocky. But soon I found out that Gorky sobbed over every poetic vest.

All the same I kept the vest. Would be happy to donate it to someone for a provincial museum.

The New Satyricon

Went through the sixty-five rubles easily and painlessly. "Pondering the prospects of a meal," started writing for *The New Satyricon*.

A Most Joyful Date

July 1915. Made the acquaintance of L. Y. and O. M. Brik.

Drafted

Got called up. By this point I didn't want to go to the front. Pretended to be a draftsman. Spent my nights with an engineer, learning to draw blueprints of automobiles. It became even harder to get published. Soldiers weren't allowed. Only Osip Brik helped me out. Bought all my poetry for fifty kopecks a line. Printed "The Backbone Flute" and "The Cloud." The cloud came out rather wispy. The censors had huffed and puffed on it. Six whole pages of dots.

Ever since then I've hated periods. Commas too.

Soldier Blues

An awful time. Drew portraits of bigwigs to get out of fighting. "War and the Universe" was unfolding in my mind, and in my heart, "Man."

1916

Finished "War and the Universe." A bit later, "Man." Printed excerpts in *The Chronicle*. Insolently shirked my military duties.

February 26, 1917

Went with the automobiles to the Duma. Got into Rodzianko's office. Looked Miliukov over. He didn't say anything, but for some reason it still seemed like he was stuttering. After an hour, I got bored. Left. Took command of the Auto School for a few days. Guchkov was in the air. The old officers took to strutting about the Duma just like in the old days. It was clear to me: soon after this revolution, the socialists would take charge. The Bolsheviks. In the first days of the revolution I wrote the chronicle-in-verse "The Revolution." Gave lectures—"The Bolsheviks of Art."

August

Russia was starting to get sick of Kerensky. Losing respect. I left *New Life*. Started thinking about *Mystery-Bouffe*.

October

To accept or not to accept the revolution? There was never any question for me (or for the other Moscow Futurists). This was my revolution. Went to Smolny. Worked. Did whatever was needed. The committee meetings started.

January

Went to Moscow. Gave readings. Nights at the Poets' Café on Nastasinsky—the revolutionary grandmother of today's little poetry salons. Wrote film scripts. Acted in the films myself. Drew posters for the cinema. June. Petersburg again.

1918

The RSFSR couldn't afford to worry about art. But that's exactly what I was worried about. Went to the Proletcult at Kschessinskaya's.

Why didn't I rejoin the party? The communists had to work on the front lines. In the arts and in education at that time, it was mainly opportunists. They would have sent me to Astrakhan to fish.

October 25, 1918

Finished the mystery. Gave readings. Lots of buzz. Meyerhold and Malevich produced it. It provoked a frightful roar. Especially from the faux-communist intelligentsia. Andreeva stopped at nothing to keep it from being staged. It got three performances—then they smashed it to bits. And the *Macbeths* started up again.

1919

Toured factories with the mystery and other works by me and my comrades. Enthusiastic reception. Organized a comfut in the Vyborg region, published *Art of the Commune*. The Academy was on the point of collapse. Moved to Moscow in the spring.

Head seized by "150,000,000." Went to work in agitation at Rosta.

1920

Finished "One Hundred Fifty Million." Printed it anonymously. Wanted everyone to add to it and improve it. No one did, though, and everyone knew who had written it. Oh well. Printing it under my own name here.

Days and nights at Rosta. All kinds of Denikins were approaching. Wrote and drew. Did about three thousand posters and six thousand captions.

1921

Fighting my way through all the red tape, the hatred, the paperwork, and the stupidity—staged a revised version of the mystery. It played at the First RSFSR Theater with Meyerhold directing and with set design by Lavinsky, Khrakovsky, and Kiseliov, and then in German translation at a circus for the Third Comintern Congress. Granovsky, Altman, and Ravdel staged it there. Played about a hundred times.

Started writing for *The News*.

1922

Organized the publishing house MAF. Gathered together Futurists and communists. Aseyev, Tretiakov, and other comrades-in-arms arrived from the Far East. Started committing to paper "The Fifth International," which I had been working on for three years. A utopia. Showed what art would be like in five hundred years.

1923

Organized Lef. Lef took on the great social theme with all the artillery of Futurism. Of course, that's not an exhaustive definition—I refer all interested parties to the pages of our journal. We rallied together tightly: Brik, Aseyev, Kushner, Arvatov, Tretiakov, Rodchenko, Lavinsky.

I wrote "About That." On our common day-to-day life, but based on personal motifs. Started thinking about the long poem "Lenin." One of our mottos, one of Lef's great conquests, was the de-aestheticization of artistic production—constructivism. Applied poetry: agitprop and domestic agitprop—advertising. Despite all the hullabaloo from other poets, I consider "Nowhere else but Mosselprom" to be poetry of the highest qualification.

1924

"Monument to the Workers of Kursk." Numerous lectures across the USSR about Lef. "Jubilee"—addressed to Pushkin. Plus other poems of this type—a cycle. Travels: Tbilisi, Yalta, Sevastopol. "Tamara and the Demon," etc. Finished the long poem "Lenin." Read it at many workers' gatherings. Was very afraid of the poem at first, as it would have been easy to descend to the level of simple political paraphrase. But the reaction of working audiences reassured me, affirming my belief in the poem's necessity. Traveled a lot abroad. European technology, industrialism, all sorts of attempts to unite them with the still impassable, former Russia—this was the idée fixe of the Futurist-Lefist.

Despite the journal's disheartening print runs, *Lef* widened its sphere of activity.

We knew that the print-run figures only indicated a lack of interest in individual journals on the part of the enormous and cold-blooded mechanism of the State Publishing House.

1925

Wrote the long agitational poem "The Flying Proletarian" and the collection of agit-poetry "Stroll Across the Heavens Yourself."

Traveled round the world. The beginning of this voyage formed the basis of a long poem (made up of shorter poems) on the theme of Paris. Planned and intended to switch from poetry to prose. Should have finished my first novel that year.

Didn't quite make it "round the world." First of all, got robbed in Paris, and second, after half a year away from home, I shot like a bullet back to the USSR. Didn't even go to San Francisco (was invited to give a lecture there). Journeyed across Mexico, the USA, and parts of France and Spain. Resulting books: publicistic prose—*My Discovery of America*—and poetry—"Spain," "The Atlantic Ocean," "Havana," "Mexico City," "America."

Finished the novel in my head, but didn't transfer it to paper, because while working on it, I became filled with a hatred of all things made up, and began to demand of myself that everything be based on names, on facts. Actually, this applies also to 1926 and 27.

1926

In my work I consciously transformed myself into a newspaperman. Feuilletons, slogans. Poets booed and hooted, but they couldn't have done journalistic work themselves—they just got printed in irresponsible little supplements. Their lyrical nonsense amused me—here's something that's easy to do, but holds no interest for anyone besides the poet's wife.

Wrote for *The News, Labor, Working Moscow, Dawn of the East, The Baku Worker,* and others.

Second job—continued the broken-off tradition of the troubadours and minstrels. Toured cities and gave readings. Novocherkassk, Vinnitsa, Kharkov, Paris, Rostov, Tbilisi, Berlin, Kazan, Sverdlovsk, Tula, Prague, Leningrad, Moscow, Voronezh, Yalta, Yevpatoria, Vyatka, Ufa, etc., etc., etc.

1927

Reestablished Lef (there was an attempt to shut it down), now called New Lef. Our basic position: against fiction, aestheticization, and psychologism in art—for agitation, qualified publicistic prose, and chronicles. Worked mainly for *Komsomolskaya Pravda*, with "Very Good" as an extracurricular.

"Very Good" I consider a programmatic piece, something like "The Cloud in Pants" was for its time. Restriction of abstract poetic devices (hyperbole, the vignette-like image as something valuable in and of itself) and invention of new devices for the treatment of chronological and agitational material. Ironic pathos in the description of trifles, but trifles that could represent a step in the right direction ("the cheese isn't moldy—lamps are burning, prices are cut"); the introduction of facts of varying historical caliber which belong together only on the order of personal associations ("Conversation with Blok," "I was told by a quiet Jew, Pavel Ilyich Lavut").

I will continue developing and implementing these plans.

Also: wrote screenplays and children's books.

Also continued my minstrelsy. Have collected about twenty thousand notes and questions from audiences at my readings, planning a book called "The Universal Answer" (to those who wrote in questions). I know what the reading public thinks about.

1928

Writing the poem "Bad." Plus a play and my literary autobiography. A lot of people have told me: "Your autobiography isn't very serious." They're right. I haven't yet gone academic and am not used to nannying my persona, and anyway, my business interests me only insofar as I can have fun with it. The rise and fall of literary trends, Symbolists, realists, etc., our struggle with them—all this I saw with my own eyes: it is a part of our very serious history. It demands to be written about. And write I will.

The Early Years
✦ 1912–1916 ✦

NIGHT

The crimson and white is wadded up and discarded,
handfuls of ducats thrown into the green,
and into the gathered-round windows' black palms
burning yellow cards have been dealt.

The boulevards and square found it not strange
to see buildings covered in dark-blue togas,
and like yellow wounds, the streetlights fastened
bangles around running pedestrians' legs.

The crowd, a quick and calico cat,
drifted on, squirming, drawn toward doorways;
everyone wanted to drag in at least a bit
of bulk from the wad of outpoured laughter.

When I felt the beckoning paws of a dress,
I rammed a smile right into their eyes; startling
as hammer blows against tin, black men guffawed,
above each brow a painted parrot wing.

1912

MORNING

The gloomy rain squinted its eyes.
Behind
the array
of clear
steel cable thoughts,
a featherbed.
And on
it
lightly rest the feet
of rising stars.
But the dy-
ing streetlamps,
tsars
in crowns of gas,
only made the eye
hurt more to see
the bickering bouquet of boulevard prostitutes.
The frightful,
biting laughter
of jokes
rises
up from toxic
yellow roses
in a zigzag.
Past the din
and horror
the eye is glad
to look:
the slave
on his crossroads,

suffering-calm-indifferent,
and the coffins
of brothels
cast by the east into one flaming vase.

1912

The
street.
Great
Danes'
faces
sharp-
er
than years.
Ov-
er
the iron horses,
out of the windows of buildings running by,
the first cubes have already leapt.
You belfry-necked swans,
stoop in your nooses of streetcar cables!
Up in the sky a giraffe sketch is ready
to color its rusty bangs.
Mottled like a trout
is the son
of the patternless field.
A conjurer,
hidden behind clock-tower dials,
draws rails
from the streetcar's mouth.
We are conquered!
Baths.
Showers.
Elevators.
The soul's bodice is unlaced.
Hands burn its body.

Cry all you want,
"This isn't what I meant!"—
sharp
are the taut straps
of torment.
The wind with its thorns
rips out
of the chimney
a tuft of smoky fur.
A bald streetlamp
lasciviously strips away
the street's
black stocking.

1913

COULD YOU?

I splattered the pattern of weekdays at once
with color splashed out from a glass;
I showed you, on a dish of aspic,
the slanting cheekbones of the ocean.
Upon the scales of a tin fish
I read the calls of new lips.
And how about you,
could you
play a nocturne
on a flute of drainpipes?

1913

ME

1

Along the road
of my deep-rutted soul,
harsh phrases' heels
weave madmen's paces.
Where cities
are hanged
and in a noose of cloud
the crooked necks
of towers
have grown stiff—
I go
alone to cry
for the policemen
crucified
on their crossroads.

2
A Few Words About My Wife

Along the distant beach of unknown seas
walks the moon,
my wife.
My redheaded mistress.
Behind her equipage,
a throng of constellations, motley-striped, stretches
    screaming.
She's crowned by an automobile garage,
kissed by newspaper kiosks,

and her gown-train's Milky Way, like some blinking errand-boy,
is decked in tinselly sparkles.
What about me?
As I burn, the yoke of my eyebrows delivers
icy buckets drawn from the wells of my eyes.
You hang there draped in lake-silks,
your thighs singing like an amber violin.
Down to the realms of the rooftops' spite
you can't cast your sparkling line.
I'm drowning in boulevards, washed over by the longing of
    sands:
don't you see, it's your daughter—
my song
in fishnet stockings
outside the cafés!

3

A Few Words About My Mama

I have a mama on wallpaper of cornflower blue.
Whereas I stroll about in motley peahens;
I torment shaggy daisies, measuring them with my stride.
Evening strikes up a tune on rusty oboes.
I walk up to the window,
believing
that I will again see
a storm cloud
seated
on top of the house.
While in my sick mama's room,
the rustle of the people runs around
from the bed to the empty corner.
Mama knows—
it's a bunch of crazy ideas

crawling out from behind the rooftops of Shustov's factory.
And when my forehead, crowned by a felt hat,
is bloodied by the dimming window-frame,
I'll say,
parting the wind's howl with my bass:
"Mama.
If I should take pity
on the vase of your torment,
knocked down by the clouds' dancing heels,
who would caress the golden hands
wrung by the billboard outside Avanzo's windows?"

4
A Few Words About Me Myself

I like to watch children die.
Have you ever noticed the hazy waves of laughter
breaking behind the proboscis of ennui?
Whereas I,
in the reading room of the streets,
have leafed back and forth through the coffin-tome.
Midnight
with its soaking wet fingers groped
me
and a broken-down fence,
and with the downpour's drops on the bald-spot of its cupola,
the crazy cathedral galloped off.
I can see that Christ has escaped from his icon—
street-sludge, weeping, kisses
the windblown hem of his tunic.
I shout at the bricks,
I thrust the dagger of frenzied words
into the swollen sky's flesh:
"Sun!

My father!
You, at least, take pity and don't torture me!
It's my blood, spilled by you, that flows down this earthly
  road.
It's my soul,
like shreds of torn cloud
in a burnt-out sky,
on the rusted cross of the belfry!
Time!
You, at least, crippled icon-dauber,
paint my visage
into the freak of the century's image-case!
I am alone, like the one remaining eye
of a man on his way to join the blind!"

1913

LOVE

A girl shyly wrapped herself up in a swamp
as frog motifs ominously swelled all around;
on the tracks, some sort of reddish figure wavered,
and locomotives in curls passed by in reproach.

On cloud couples, through the sun's caustic fumes,
the fury of a mazurka of wind was engraved,
and here I am—a sultrified July sidewalk,
and a woman throws me cigarette-butt kisses!

Abandon your cities, you stupid people!
Go forth naked in the sun, to pour
drunken wines into your wineskin-breasts
and rain-kisses onto your coal cheeks.

1913

We crawl under the earth's fallen-out palm eyelashes
to poke out the walleyes of deserts,
or on the shriveled lips of canals
to catch dreadnoughts' smiles.
Cool off, spite!
I won't let you lift my wild, decrepit mother
onto the bonfire of blazed constellations.
Road—horn of hell—inebriate the snores of the cargo wagons!
Widen with intoxication the volcanoes' smoking nostrils!
We'll throw molting angels' feathers onto our loved ones' hats,
we'll chop tails for our boas from comets hobbling into space.

1913

THE GIANT HELL OF THE CITY

Windows shattered the giant hell of the city
into minuscule hellikins, suckling with lights.
Automobiles, the red devils, rose up,
blasting their horns right in your ear.

And there, under the billboard for Kerch herring—
a knocked-down old fogey fumbled for his glasses
and burst into tears when, in the evening whirlwind,
a streetcar got a running start and flung up its pupils.

In gaps between skyscrapers, where ore was blazing
and the iron of trains piled up on a manhole—
an airplane gave a brief shout and crashed
where the wounded sun's eye was oozing out.

And only then, wadding up its blanket of streetlamps,
night loved itself out, lewd and drunken,
and behind the suns of streets, somewhere there hobbled,
worthless to everyone, a flabby moon.

1913

TAKE THAT!

An hour from now, your flaccid fat will flow,
man by man, out onto the clean street,
and here I've revealed to you so many boxes of verse,
I—the spendthrift and prodigal of priceless words.

You there, man, you've got cabbage in your mustache
from some half-eaten, unfinished soup somewhere;
you there, woman, your white makeup's so thick,
you peer out like an oyster from a shell of things.

All of you will pile up on the butterfly of the poet's heart,
dirty, in galoshes and without galoshes.
The crowd will go nuts, rubbing against itself,
bristling its little legs, the hundred-headed louse.

And if today I, a crude Hun,
should be disinclined to make faces for you—well, then
I'll burst out laughing and spit with joy,
spit in your faces,
I—the prodigal and spendthrift of priceless words.

1913

THEY DON'T UNDERSTAND ANYTHING

Walked into a barbershop and said, perfectly calm,
"Would you be so kind as to give my ears a trim?"
The smooth-shaven barber immediately bristled,
made a long face, like a pear's.
"Madman!
Clown!"—
the words started jumping.
Foul language rushed about from chirp to chirp,
and for a lo-o-o-o-ng time
someone's head kept giggling,
yanked up out of the crowd like an old radish.

1913

"What a charming night!"
"That one
(pointing at a girl),
from yesterday,
is it the same one?"
On the sidewalk someone said:
"post—
the tires jumped—
office."
The city suddenly turned inside out.
A drunk climbed on top of some hats.
Billboards gaped wide their fright,
spitting out,
now *O,*
now *S.*
And on top of the hill,
where dark tears were falling,
where the shy city
had clambered,
it suddenly seemed true:
a flabby *O*
and disgustingly obedient *S.*

1913

THE FOP'S BLOUSE

I'll sew myself black trousers
from the velvet of my voice.
A yellow blouse from ten feet of sunset.
On the Nevsky Avenue of the world, along its polished lanes,
I'll stroll at the pace of a Don Juan and a fop.

Let the earth cry out, having turned womanish in peace:
"You're on your way to rape green springs!"
I'll cast at the sun, with an impudent grin:
"On the asphalt's smooth surface I enjoy burring my *r*'s!"

Is it not because the sky is blue,
and the earth is my mistress in this festive cleansing,
that I present you with verses, fun as bee-bah-bo,
sharp and necessary, like toothpicks!

All you women who love my meat, and this
girl here, who's looking at me as at a brother,
bespatter me, the poet, with smiles—
I'll sew them with flowers onto my fop's blouse!

1914

Listen up!
After all, if they light up the stars,
does that mean anyone cares?
Does that mean someone wants them to be there?
Does that mean someone calls these little gobs of spit pearls?

And, floundering
in the blizzards of midday dust,
storms in to see God,
fears he's too late,
cries,
kisses the veiny hand,
begs—
please, there absolutely must be a star—
swears
he'll never endure this starless torture!
And afterward,
walks around anxious
but calm on the outside.
Says to someone:
"You're okay now, right?
Not afraid?
Yes?!"
Listen up!
After all, if they light up
the stars,

does that mean anyone cares?
Does that mean it's necessary
that every evening
above the rooftops
at least one star should light up?!

1914

The street has caved in like the nose of a syphilitic.
The river is pure lechery leaked out in drool.
Having stripped off their skivvies, to the last little leaflet,
the gardens indecently sprawl across June.

I step out on the square,
placing a burnt-out
city block on my head like a red wig.
The people are frightened—dangling from my mouth,
a shout, partly chewed, is still wagging its legs.

But I won't be berated, but I won't be condemned—
like a prophet's, my path will be strewn with flowers.
All these people, the ones with the caved-in noses, know:
I am your poet.

Your Judgment Day scares me about as much as a tavern!
Prostitutes will carry me forth like a sacred relic,
carry me alone through the burning buildings
and show me to God in their own justification.

And God will break down in tears over my little book!
No words—just convulsions stuck together in a wad;
he'll run around the sky with my poems tucked in his armpit,
and, panting for breath, read them to his acquaintances.

1914

PETERSBURG AGAIN

In the ears were snippets of a warm ball,
but from the north—more hoary than snow—
a fog with the bloodthirsty face of a cannibal
chewed unsavory people.

A clock hung in the air like crude swearing;
six loomed after five.
And some kind of garbage looked down from the sky,
majestically, like Leo Tolstoy.

1914

MAMA AND THE EVENING KILLED BY THE GERMANS

Along the black streets, white mothers
spasmodically spread, like brocade on a coffin.
They wept their way into the crowd shouting about the
                                                    beaten enemy:
"Ach, shut their eyes, shut the newspapers' eyes!"

A letter.

Mama, louder!
Smoke.
Smoke.
More smoke!
What's that you're mumbling, Mama, to me?
Don't you see—
The air is paved
with stone rumbling under artillery fire!
Ma-a-a-ma!
They just brought in an evening all covered in wounds.
He held on for a long time,
spread too tight,
rough around the edges,
and suddenly—
his cloud shoulders broke down;
he burst into tears, the poor guy, on Warsaw's breast.
The stars, on their hankies of dark-blue cotton,
screeched out:
"He's killed,
my dear,
my dear one!"

And the new moon's eye squinted terribly
at the dead fist clenching a cartridge clip.
Lithuanian villages gathered round to watch,
as Kaunas, forged by a kiss into one giant stump,
bringing tears to the golden eyes of its churches,
wrung its street-fingered hands.
But the evening cried out,
legless,
armless:
"You've got it all wrong,
I'm still quite able—
ha!—
clanging my spurs in a burning mazurka,
to twirl my golden-brown mustache!"

The doorbell.

What's wrong,
Mama?
White, white as brocade on a coffin.
"Leave me alone!
It's about him,
he's been killed—a telegram.
Ach, shut their eyes,
shut the newspapers' eyes!"

1914

The violin was beside herself with begging
and suddenly burst out
so like a child
that the drum couldn't hold back anymore:
"Very good, very good, very good!"
But he was tired
and didn't stick around for the violin's speech—
he stepped out onto dazzling Kuznetsky
and was off.
The orchestra looked on like strangers
as the violin cried her heart out
without words,
without tact,
only somewhere
a stupid cymbal
clanged out:
"What's that?
How's that?"
And when the helicon,
copper-faced,
sweaty,
shouted:
"Fool!
Crybaby!
Use a hankie!"—
I got up,
made my way, reeling, through the sheet music,
through the music stands stooped in horror,
and for some reason shouted:
"My God!"

Threw my arms around her wooden neck:
"You know what, violin?
We're awfully alike:
I also bawl—
but I can't prove a thing!"
The musicians had a laugh:
"He's really stepped in it!
Come home to his wooden bride!
What a head case!"
But I couldn't care less!
I'm a good guy.
"You know what, violin?
Let's—
let's live together!
Ah?"

1914

Well, this is completely unbearable!
I really am bitten to shreds by spite.
I'm angry not in the way you might be:
like a dog, I'd take that barebrow moon's face—
I'd up and
howl it to pieces.

Nerves, I guess . . .
I'll step out,
take a walk.
But even outside, I didn't calm down, not a bit.
Some woman shouted something about a good evening.
I knew I had to answer,
because she was an acquaintance.
And I wanted to,
but I sensed—
I couldn't answer like a human.

What was this ridiculous outrage!
Was I asleep, or what?
I patted myself:
I was the same as ever,
with the same face I'd grown used to.
I touched my lip,
and beneath my lip I felt it—
a fang.

Quickly I covered my face, as if I were blowing my nose.
Made a dash for the house, doubling my pace.
As I carefully skirted the police booth,

suddenly there was a deafening shout:
"Police!
It's a tail!"

I ran my hand over myself—and was dumbfounded!
This,
plainer than any fangs,
I hadn't even noticed in my feverish gallop:
from beneath my jacket
an enormous tail fanned out
and coiled behind me,
big and canine.

What now?
Someone roared out, drawing a crowd.
To the second person were added a third, a fourth.
They crushed an old woman;
crossing herself, she yelled something about the devil.

And when, bristling their whisker-twigs in my face,
the crowd fell on me,
enormous,
wicked,
I got down on all fours
and barked out:
Woof! Woof! Woof!

1915

Tobacco smoke has eaten through the air.
The room
is a chapter out of Kruchenykh's hell.
Remember—
just past that window,
in a frenzy
I first
caressed your hands.
Today you're sitting there,
heart wrapped in metal.
Another day
and you'll throw me out,
perhaps with a curse.
In the dim front hallway, my arm, wracked with trembles,
will take a long time to get into my sleeve.
I'll run outside,
throw my body into the street.
I'll lose my mind,
wild,
lashed by despair.
Let's not do that,
my darling,
my dear,
let's say our good-byes now.
All the same
my love—
such a heavy weight—
hangs on you
wherever you go.
Let me roar out in one final shout

the bitterness of resentful complaints.
If you manage to drive a bull to exhaustion,
he'll leave,
he'll sprawl in the cool waters.
Apart from your love,
for me
there's no sea,
and your love offers no respite—no use in tearful pleading.
If an elephant gets tired and longs for peace,
he'll lie down regally in the fiery sands.
Apart from your love,
for me
there's no sun,
and I don't even know where you are, or with whom.
If you were to wear out a poet this way,
he'd
trade his beloved for money and fame,
but for me
there is no joyful sound
apart from the sound of your beloved name.
I won't throw myself down the stairs
and I won't drink poison;
I won't pull the trigger with a gun to my head.
Apart from your gaze,
there isn't a blade that has power over me.
Tomorrow you'll forget
that I crowned you,
that I seared with love my flowering soul,
and the whirling carnival of empty days
will tatter the pages of my books . . .
Will the dry leaves of my words
force people to stop,
gasping for breath?

Let me, at least,
as a final act of tenderness, pave
your parting path.

May 26, 1916, Petrograd

TO HIS BELOVED SELF THE AUTHOR DEDICATES THESE LINES

Six words.
Heavy as hammer blows.
"Caesar's unto Caesar, God's unto God."
But where
is someone like me
to go?
Where has a lair been prepared for me?

If only I were
small,
like the Pacific Ocean—
I'd stand on the waves' tiptoes,
snuggle up to the moon on the tide.
Where am I to find a beloved,
one who's like me?
She wouldn't fit in the tiny sky!

If only I were poor!
Like a billionaire!
What's money to the soul?
She's got an insatiable thief inside.
For the unbridled horde of my desires
all the gold of all the Californias wouldn't suffice.

Oh, to be tongue-tied
like Dante
or Petrarch!
To light my soul ablaze for one woman!
To order it to smolder away in verse!
My words

and my love
would be a triumphal arch:
through it
the mistresses of all the ages would pass,
pass with great pomp—and without a trace.

Oh, if only I were
quiet,
like thunder,
I'd whimper
and wrack the earth's decrepit cloister with tremors.
If
with all my might
I howled out in full voice—
comets would wring their burning hands
and hurl themselves down in anguish.

I'd devour nights with the rays of my eyes—
oh, if only I were
dim
like the sun!
That's the last thing I need—
to slake with my shining
the earth's emaciated little bosom!

I'll move on,
dragging my enormous love.
In what night,
what delirious,
ailing night,
and by what Goliaths was I conceived—
so big
and so useless?

1916

The Years of Upheaval

✦ 1917–1920 ✦

OUR MARCH

Pound the steps of rebellion into the squares!
Raise higher the bank of proud heads!
Spilling over in a second great flood,
we'll wash the cities of worlds.

Piebald is the bull of days.
Slow, the cart of years.
Running is our God.
Our heart is a drum.

Is there a gold more heavenly than ours?
Can we be stung by the wasp of a bullet?
Our weapon—our songs.
Our gold—ringing voices.

Lie down in greenery, meadow:
pave the floor of days.
Rainbow, lend your arched shaft-bows
to the swift horses of years.

You see, the sky of stars is bored!
We'll weave our songs without it.
Hey, Great Bear! Demand that we
be taken to heaven alive.

Drink up joy! Sing!
Spring is spilled in our veins.
Heart, strike the beat!
Our breast is the copper of kettledrums.

1917

BEING GOOD TO HORSES

Hooves were pounding.
As if singing:
"Grip.
Grab.
Grope.
Group."

Wind-drunk,
ice-shod,
the street slipped and slid.
Onto its croup
the horse fell with a crash,
and straightaway
gawker after gawker—
come to Kuznetsky to bell-bottom along—
crowded round.
Laughter jingled and jangled:
"The horse fell!"
"A horse fell!"
Kuznetsky laughed.
I alone
withheld my voice from the general howl.
I approached
and saw
the horse's eyes . . .

The street tipped over,
kept flowing along . . .
I approached and saw
drop after drop, enormous drops,

roll down the snout,
disappear in the fur . . .

And some sort of universal
animal yearning
splashed out of me
and spread in a rustle.
"Horse, please don't.
Horse, listen to me––
you think this means you're somehow worse?
Kiddo,
we're all horses a little bit,
each of us is in his own way a horse."
Perhaps,
being old,
she had no need for a nanny,
or perhaps my idea struck her as coarse,
only
the horse
jerked herself up,
found her footing,
gave a neigh
and was off.
Wagging her tail.
A chestnut child.
She arrived cheerful,
took her place in the stall.
And all the while it seemed to her—
she was a young foal,
and it was worthwhile to live
and worthwhile to work.

1918

To thee,
hissed at,
mocked by whole batteries,
to thee,
in ulcers from the backbiting of bayonets,
I rapturously render up
over the soared swearwords
my ode's most solemn
"O"!
O Beastly!
O Childish!
O Halfpenny!
O Great One!
What other name have you been given?
What turns might you still take, O Two-Faced One?
A harmonious structure
or a heap of ruins?
To the engineer
covered in coal dust,
to the miner digging up layers of ore,
you sing praises,
sing praises with reverence;
you glorify human labor.
But tomorrow
the Blessed
will raise its cathedral
rafters in vain, begging for mercy—
the snub-snouted hogs of your six-inch guns
will blast away the millennia of the Kremlin.
Glory.

Wheezing through her dying voyage.
Her sirens' squeal is muffled and thin.
You send sailors
onto the sinking ship,
where
a forgotten
kitten meows.
And afterward!
You roar through the drunken crowd,
your dashing mustache all twirled up in swagger.
With rifle-butts you knock gray-haired admirals
headfirst
from the bridge in Helsingfors.
It's still licking and licking yesterday's wounds,
and again I see opened veins.
To thee I send a philistine's
"Oh be thrice cursed!"
and my own,
the poet's
"Oh be four times glorified, Blessed One!"

1918

Brigades of old fogeys are still busy spinning
their same old long-spun-out thread.
Comrades!
To the barricades!—
the barricades of hearts and souls.
The only true communist is he
who's burnt every bridge leading back.
Enough of this marching, Futurists—
it's time for a leap into the future!
It's not enough to build a steam engine—
you twist on some wheels and you're gone.
If a song doesn't thunder through the station,
then what's the use of alternating current?
Pile sound upon sound
and move forward,
singing and whistling.
There are still some good letters left:
R,
Sha,
Shcha.
It's not enough to build things in pairs,
to fluff up the edges of your trouser legs.
All the Sov-deps in the world can't move armies
if musicians don't provide a march.
Drag grand pianos out into the street,
and hang a drum out the window!
Whether it's a drum
or a piano,
just make sure there's a din—
make sure there's thunder.

What's that all about—sweating in factories,
smearing your face with soot,
and then, in your time off,
staring blankly with dreamy eyes
at other people's luxury.
Enough of halfpenny truths.
Wipe everything old from your heart.
Streets are our brushes.
Squares, our palettes.
The days of the Revolution have yet to be sung
by the thousand-paged
book of time.
To the streets, all you Futurists,
drummers, and poets!

1918

We seek the future.
We've walked across miles of paving blocks.
But we ourselves
have now settled down like a cemetery,
weighed down by the tombstones of palaces.
When you find
a White Guardsman, you put him up against the wall.
But have you forgotten Raphael?
Have you forgotten Rastrelli?
It's high time
for bullets
to tinkle across museum walls.
Fire on the old order with the hundred-inch guns of your
    gullets!
Sow death in the enemy's camp.
Don't let us catch you, hirelings of capital.
Is that Tsar Alexander
standing
on Insurrection Square?
Send dynamite!
We lined up cannons at the edge of the forest,
deaf to the White Guard's caresses.
But why
has Pushkin not been attacked?
And the other
generals of classicism?
We protect the old order in the name of art.
Or has the Revolution's tooth
gone dull chewing on crowns?
Hurry up!

Spew smoke over the Winter Palace—
from a macaroni factory!
So we shot for a day or two from our guns,
and we thought
we'd clobber the old.
What's that!
To replace the jacket from the outside
is not enough, comrades!
Turn it inside out!

1918

THE POET WORKER

People yell at the poet:
"I'd like to see you standing at a lathe.
What's poetry?
It's worthless!
I guess you don't have the guts for real work."
Maybe
labor
to us
is dearer than any other pursuits.
I too am a factory.
And if I lack smokestacks,
then maybe
for me
without smokestacks it's harder.
I know—
you have no love for idle phrases.
You chop down an oak in the name of work.
But are we
not also woodworkers?
We work the oaks of people's heads.
Of course,
it's an honorable thing—to fish.
To haul in the net.
Let there be sturgeons!
But poets' labor—even more honorable—
is to catch living people, rather than fish.
It's enormous labor to burn over a forge,
to temper the hissing pieces of iron.
But who could
accuse us of idleness?

We file down brains with the rasp of our tongue.
Who's higher—the poet
or the technician
who
leads people to material gains?
Both.
Hearts, too, are motors.
The soul, too, is a most clever engine.
We are equals.
Comrades in the working masses.
Proletarians in body and spirit.
Only together
can we decorate the universe
and set the world banging in marches.
We'll fence ourselves in from the verbal storms with a jetty.
Get to it!
Work is alive and new.
As for idle orators—
onto the mill!
To the millers with them!
They'll turn millstones with the water of their speeches.

1918

AN EXTRAORDINARY ADVENTURE WHICH BEFELL VLADIMIR MAYAKOVSKY IN THE SUMMER AT A DACHA

(Pushkino, Akulova hill, Rumiantsev's dacha,
eighteen miles down the Yaroslavl railroad)

Like one hundred forty suns the sunset blazed
as summer rolled into July;
the weather was hot,
heat shimmered and swam—
this took place at a dacha.
The knoll of Pushkino hunched up
against Akulova hill,
and at the foot of the hill
was a village—
its rind of rooftops grimaced.
Beyond the village
was a hollow,
and down into that hollow
the sun descended every night,
faithfully and slowly.
Come morning, once again
to flood
the world,
the scarlet sun would rise.
And day by day,
this started
to annoy
me
terribly.
And one day, flying into such a rage

that everything went pale in fear,
I shouted point-blank at the sun:
"Get down!
enough with the traipsing, you hear?!"
I shouted at the sun:
"You freeloader!
You're up there coddled in clouds,
but down here,
you can forget about winter and summer—
just sit and draw your posters!"
I shouted at the sun:
"Hold it!
listen up, goldilobe:
don't just drop idly
from the sky—
drop by
my place for tea!"
What have I done!
I'm a dead man!
Straight toward me,
of its own free will,
the sun itself,
with sunbeam strides,
steps down into the field.
I try not to reveal my fright
as I withdraw butt-first.
Its eyes are in the garden now.
It's passing through the garden.
Invading windows,
doors,
and cracks,
the sun's mass tumbled and
burst in;
pausing to catch its breath,

it began in a bass:
"I'm whipping my fires backward
for the first time since creation.
You invited me, right?
Whip up some tea,
poet, whip up some jam!"
The sun itself shed a tear—
the heat was enough to drive you crazy—
but I just pointed to the samovar
and said,
"Take a seat, then,
luminary!"
The devil must have egged me on
to yell at it the way I did;
embarrassed,
I sat down on a corner of the bench
and fretted—lest things get any worse!
But from the sun there flowed a strange
lume—
and forgoing
staidness,
I sat there warming to
our conversation gradually.
I talked of this
and talked of that,
said Rosta was really wearing me down,
to which the sun retorted:
"C'mon,
don't grieve—
just look at things simply!
You think
it's easy
for me to shine?
Why don't you go and try it!

But here's the thing:
you chose to go,
so you go—and shine wide open!"
We chattered on like that till dark—
that is, till the time formerly known as night.
No chance of darkness now!
We spoke
on quite familiar terms.
And soon,
making no secret of our friendship,
I slapped the sun's shoulder.
It felt the same:
"You and I,
comrade—we're quite the pair!
Let's go, poet,
and blaze
and laud
in the gray rubbish of the world.
I will pour out the sun that's mine,
and you, your own,
in verse."
The wall of shadows,
the prison of nights
fell to the double-barrel sun.
Bustle of poetry and light,
shine anywhere you can!
If the other one gets tired,
and night tries
to snuggle up—
that stupid sleepyhead—
suddenly I'll
dawn with all my might—
and day will ring out anew.
To shine always,

to shine all-wheres,
until the end of days,
to shine—
and that's all there is to it!
My slogan
and the sun's!

1920

The Soviet Years

✦ 1922–1930 ✦

ALL MEETINGED OUT

The moment night turns into dawn,
every day I see them:
some to Main,
some to Comm,
some to Polit,
some to Enlight—
the people head off to their departments.
A rain of paper files pours down
the moment they step into the building:
picking out about fifty—
the most important ones!—
the civil servants set off for their meetings.

You show up in some office:
"Could he perhaps grant me audience?
I've been coming since the dawn of time."
"Comrade Ivan Vanych has left for a meeting—
a joint session of the Theater Division and the Horse
    Breeders."

You travel a hundred staircases.
The world is unkind.
And the same thing happens again:
"He said to come back in an hour.
He's at a meeting
concerning the purchase of a bottle of ink
by the District Co-op."

One hour later:
neither the secretary

nor his secretary is anywhere to be found—
it's just bare!
Everyone under twenty-two years of age
is at the Communist Youth meeting.

Once more I ascend, looking up at the night,
to the top floor of a seven-story building.
"Is Comrade Ivan Vanych back yet?"
"He's at a meeting
of the A-B-C-D Commissariat."

In a fury,
I storm into their meeting
like an avalanche,
belching out wild curses on the way.
And I see:
it's just halves of people sitting there.
Oh, devilry!
Where the hell is the other half?
"They've been sliced up!
Murdered!"
I rush about, shouting.
My reason recoils from the terrifying scene.
And I hear
the perfectly calm little voice of the secretary:
"They're at two meetings at once.
In a day
we have about twenty meetings
to attend.
Whether we like it or not, we have to split double.
Below the belt's here,
and the rest,
somewhere else."

With all the excitement, you can't fall asleep.
It's early morning;
I greet the dawn with a dream:
"Oh, how about
just
one more meeting
regarding the eradication of all meetings!"

1922

The wind was howling and knew not about whom,
inspiring trembling in our heart.
Along the tracks walked a peasant woman with milk,
along the railroad tracks.

But at seven o'clock sharp, in due form,
tearing in full career from the Oka,
its lights flashing behind the signal-posts,
an express train takes off.

The woman would have been mutilated—
in vain the hundred whistles bellowed—
but a peasant man with mutton was there,
and let her know just in time.

To the right went the woman,
to the left went the train.
If not for the man, it would have
cut her in half at the waist.

The smoke has now disappeared behind the stars;
the woman and man are gone.
We will pay tribute to our hero,
winging up above the workweek.

Though he came from the dregs of the nation,
he saved her in broad daylight.
Long live the average guy
who trades in mutton!

Let the sun shine in the darkness!
Burn, you stars, at night!
And long live both these and those—
and everyone else besides!

1923

Alexander Sergeyevich,
                    allow me to introduce myself.
                                        Mayakovsky.
Give me your hand!
                    Here's my rib cage.
                                        Listen—
                                        not a heartbeat, but a moan;
I worry about it,
                    this lion cub subdued into a doggy.
I never knew
                    there were so many
                                        thousand tons
in my
        shamefully frivolous noggin.
I'm dragging you off.
                    That must catch you unawares.
Too firm a handshake?
                    Did I hurt you?
                                        Pardon me, dear fellow.
You and I
        both have
                    eternity to spare.
What's it to us
            to lose
                    an hour or two?!
Just like water—
                let's
                    babble as we rush along,
just like spring—
                unfettered
                        and free!

In the sky up there
                    the moon's
                              so young
that to let her out
                    without chaperones
                                        would be risky.
I'm
    now
        free
            from love
                      and from posters.
Like a mere pelt of jealousy
                             lies the bear,
                                            sharp-clawed.
You can
        see for yourself
                          that the earth is slanted—
sit down
         on your butt
                       and slide!
No,
    I won't foist myself on anyone
                                    in my dark little *melancholishka*,
and anyway, there's no one
                           I feel like talking to.
It's just that
               the gills of rhyme
                                   bristle a bit quicker
for guys like us
                 on the poetic sand.
Dreams can be harmful,
                       and reverie's no use,

you have
            to keep up
                        that workaday drudgery.
But sometimes—
                        life
                        rises up in a different view,
and you understand
                        the big picture
                                    by way of nonsense.
Many times now
                        we've stuck
                                    our bayonets
                                                in lyricism;
we seek a speech
                        precise
                                    and bare.
But poetry's
            the damnedest thing:
it exists—
            and we can't make heads or tails of it.
Take this,
            for example—
                        is it spoken or bleated?
A blue snout
            with orange whiskers,
like some biblical
                        Nebuchadnezzar—
Sug-Co-op.
Bring us some glasses!
                        I know
                                    it's oldfangled
to drown grief
            in booze,

but look—
                                   from
Red and **White Stars**
                         are weighing anchor
in a flurry
            of assorted visas.
It's nice here with you—
                              I'm glad
                                   you're at my table.
The Muse
            sure could winkle it out of you.
What is it
            your
                  Olga used to say? . . .
No, not Olga!
                  It's from Onegin's
                                   letter to Tatiana.
He's like,
            "Your husband's
                              a fool
                                   and an old cretin,
I love you,
            be mine without fail;
right now
            in the morning I must be certain
I'll see you in the afternoon."
Been there, done that:
                              the standing under windows,
the letters,
            the nervous jelly of jitters.
But see,
            when
                  you're not even able to feel sorrow—

that,
     Alexander Sergeyich,
               is a lot harder to take.
Come along, Mayakovsky!
             May-ake your way south!
Wrest out
     your heart in rhymes—
there,
    love too is kaput,
my dear Vladim Vladimych.
No,
   the problem isn't old age, I say!
Goading
     forward my carcass,
with pleasure
        I could handle two others
              in a fracas,
and if I get mad—
        even three.
They say
I'm too i-n-d-i-v-i-d-u-a-l-i-s-t-i-c in my choice of themes!
Let's keep that *entre nous* . . .
           (so the censor doesn't cut me off).
I'll pass it on—
      they say
        they've even seen
two
  Executive Committee members
          in love!
So you see—
     they leaked a bit of gossip,
           and sate their souls with it.
Alexander Sergeyich,

    don't you listen
        to them!
Perhaps
   I
   alone
     truly regret
that today
    you're no longer among the living.
I wish
  we could have
     come to an understanding
        while you were alive.
Soon
  I too
    will die
     and have to keep mum.
After death
    we'll
     stand almost like neighbors:
you at P,
   and I
     at M.
Who's in between us?
     What kind of company must we keep?
When it comes to poets
     my country's
       really scraping the dregs.
What a drag—
    looks like Nadson
      wormed his way in.
We'll ask
   that he be relocated
     somewhere
      around X!

Kolya
        Nekrasov,
                on the other hand,
                        the late Alyosha's boy—
he's a cardplayer
            and a poet,
                    and not at all bad-looking.
You know him?
                Now, he's
                    a good guy.
He'll
        make us good company—
                        he can stay.
What about my contemporaries?!
We'd do just fine
                to trade away some fifty-odd
                                for you.
A man
        could crack
                his cheekbones yawning!
Dorogoichenko,
                Gerasimov,
                        Kirillov,
                            Rodov—whew!
What a
        tEDious panorama!
Okay, so there's Yesenin
                and his gang of peasant wannabes.
What a laugh!
                Cows
                    in kid gloves.
You give him a listen . . .
                        just a voice from the crowd!
With a balalaika!

A poet
      should be
            a master at life as well.
We're strong
            as the hooch in a Poltava shtoff.
Okay, but what about Bezymensky?!
                              Well . . .
he's all right, I guess . . .
            like carrot coffee.
True,
      we do
            have
                  Kolka
                  Aseyev.
That one can write.
            He's got my
                  iron grip.
But we have to do
            all this work ourselves!
A small family,
            but still a family.
If you were alive,
            we'd make you
                  coeditor of *Lef*.
I could
      even
            trust you with agitprop work.
I'd show you just once:
            "Like this," I'd say,
                  "and that . . ."
And you could do it—
            you're pretty good
                  with words.

I'd give you
            the perfume
                        and textile trust listings,
so you could advertise
                  for all those
                              department-store dames.
(I even
        tried a bit of iambic lisping,
only
    to make you feel
                    at home.)
These days
          you'd have to drop
                          your iamb-stilts.
The teeth of pitchforks
                      and bayonets
                                  are our pens—
the battles of the revolution
                          make Poltava seem silly,
and our love
            is more grandiose
                          than Onegin's.
Beware of Pushkin scholars.
                        Some Geezer-brained Pliushkin,
rusty little quill
                in hand,
                        will start raving.
"It seems," he'll say,
                  "*Lef*'s
                        got a hold
                                of Pushkin.
That Negro!
            and he dares contend
                              with Derzhavin . . ."

I like you, Pushkin—

                        but alive,

                                 not a mummy.

They've polished you up

                        with textbook lacquer.

In life,

        you too—

               I think—

must have raged and stormed.

                        You African, you!

That son of a bitch d'Anthès!

                        The high-society rogue.

We'd have asked him:

                  "And *who* might your parents have been?

What were you up to

                before 1917?"

If only we'd gotten our hands on the frog.

Anyway,

        this is starting to smack of spiritism.

                              Enough of this drivel!

So to speak,

            a slave to honor . . .

                      by a bullet struck down . . .

To this day

           there's quite a few

                    of them around—

all kinds of

           other men

                chasing our wives.

We have it good here

                in the Land of the Soviets.

One can live,

           one can labor in harmony.

It's just that,
                unfortunately,
                                we don't have any poets—
but then again,
                maybe that's how it should be.
Well, it's time:
                dawn's rays
                                are incandescing.
We wouldn't want
                the police
                                to start a manhunt.
Here on Tverskoy Boulevard
                                you're quite the landmark.
Well, c'mon,
                I'll set you
                                on your pedestal.
I'd say
        a monument in life
                        is my due by rank.
I'd stuff it full
                of dynamite and—
                                "kablooey!"
I can't stand
                anything that's dead and rank!
I adore
        everything that's full of life!

1924

TAMARA AND THE DEMON

So this is the Terek
              that has poets
                       in hysterics.
And I hadn't seen it.
                  Big loss, I'm sure.
I stepped off the bus,
              waddled
down,
     spat
          into the Terek from the shore,
poked a stick
            into its
               foamy water.
What's so great about it?
                   A total wreck!
Kicks and screams
            like Yesenin in a police station.
It seems Lunacharsky,
             on his way
                  to Borjomi,
botched the Terek's
            organization.
I want to turn up
            my insolent nose
and I feel it:
          I freeze on the verge,
I fall under the sway
            of a strange
                hypnosis,
the effervescence of water
             and foam.

That tower,
        like a revolver
                pointed at the sky's head,
strikes me down
         with its pristine beauty.
Go ahead,
        just try to subject it
                 to the chairman of the arts—
Peter Semionych
        Kogan.
And as I stand here
         the spite takes hold,
to think,
      this ragged terrain, these rock faces,
like such a talentless hack
             I
           sold
for fame,
      reviews,
         and public debates.
My place
      is not in *Red Grain Fields,*
              but here,
and not paid by the line,
         but free of charge
I should strive
     at the top of my voice to roar,
ripping out
      the strings of guitars.
I know my voice:
        the tone may be lousy,
but its furious strength
          is fearsome.

Whoever's seen it
                won't have any
                                doubts that
Tamara
        would hear me.
Though she's wound up,
                        the queen restrains herself,
majestically
            wags her finger.
But I tell her
            up front:
                        "I don't give a damn
if you're a queen
                or a laundress!
After all,
        for these songs of yours—
                                what's your fee?!
Whereas laundry
                means a kopeck for the family.
And the mountains
                    don't give away much for free:
just water—
            go ahead,
                    have a drink!"
The queen's in a fury,
                        reaches straight for her dagger.
Like a nanny goat
                shot out of a Berdan.
But you know me:
                I tell her,
                            with my customary swagger—
taking her by the arm . . .
                        courteously . . .
                                    "Ma'am!

Why blow your top
                    like a steam engine?
You and I,
                we're in the same lyrical line.
I've known you forever,
                        heard so much about you
from a certain Lermontov.
He swore
        that in passion
                    you had no equal.
You're just the way
                    I pictured you.
I'm done waiting for love,
                        I'm thirty years old.
Let's love each other.
                        Simply.
A love to make
            this cliff
                    spread flat like a fluffy bed.
I'll hide you from the devil
                        and from God!
What's the Demon to you?
                        A fantasy!
                            Nothing but a spirit!
And a bit too old for you—
                    mythology.
Be a dear,
        don't throw me into the abyss.
You think that pain's enough
                        to scare me off?
I don't
        even care
                if my jacket gets ripped,

much less
        my chest or my back.
You give
      a guy
         a good shove from here,
and he'll fall
        smack dead into the Terek.
To get thrown out
          in Moscow
            is more painful by far!
You count steps
        all the way down the staircase.
My work here is finished,
          it's not my affair.
Let Pasternak write about it,
           for all I care,
in a fury
      of corrections and inkblots.
As for us . . .
        just say yes, Tamara!"
The rest of the story
          isn't fit for books.
I'm a modest fellow,
          and I'm quitting.
The Demon himself flew down,
            eavesdropped,
               then drooped
and stalked off,
        stinking
          to no purpose.
Lermontov comes to see us,
          scorning rifts in time.
He beams,
     "What a happy pair!"

I love company.
                    A bottle of wine!
Pour a drink for the Hussar, Tamarochka dear!

1924

A FAREWELL

In the car,
          my last franc already exchanged.
"What time is the train to Marseille?"
Paris
      runs alongside,
                      seeing me off,
in all
      its impossible beauty.
Well up
        in my eyes,
                    O slush of parting,
smack
      my heart
              with sentimentality!
I should like
            to live
                    and die in Paris,
if there were no
                such land
                          as *Moscow*.

                                                    1925

I'll become,
                if not Tolstoy, then a fatty, —
all I do is eat
                and write,
                                stupefied by the heat.
Who hasn't played the philosopher while at sea?
Only water.
Yesterday
            the ocean was mad
                                as the devil,
today,
        meeker
                than a dove on her eggs.
What's the difference!
                        Everything flows,
everything changes.
Water
        has
            its own seasons:
times of ebb
                and times of flow.
But Steklov's pen
                    never runs out
                                    of water.
No fair.
A croaked fishie
                    floats all alone,
her finlets
            hanging there
                            like shot-down winglets.

She's been floating for weeks,
                    and she has
                              neither bottom
nor top.
Coming toward us
                    slower than the body of a seal
is a steamship from Mexico,
                              just where we're headed.
It couldn't be otherwise.
                    It's the division
of labor.
That's a whale, they say.
                    Perhaps they're right.
It's like a fishy version of Bedny,
                              about three times as wide.
But Demian's whiskers are on the outside,
                              whereas the whale's
are within.
Years are seagulls.
                    They fly off in formation
and hit the water
                    to cram their bellies with fishies.
The seagulls have vanished.
                    Tell me, in essence,
where are the birdies?

I was born
          and grew up;
                    they fed me a pacifier;
I've lived,
          worked,
                    and grown pretty old . . .

Now life too shall pass by
                              just like the Azorean
Islands.

July 3, 1925—the Atlantic Ocean

BROADWAY

The asphalt's like glass.
                    I jingle as I walk.
The grasses and forests
                    are shaven clean off.
The avenues run
            from south
                    to north,
and from east to west,
                the streets.
And in between—
                (right where their builders dropped them!)—
are buildings
            of impossible length.
Some
    as long
            as from here to the stars,
others,
        from here to the moon.
Your Yankee's
            not one
                to wear out his soles:
hence the regular
                and express elevator.
At seven o'clock,
                in comes the human tide,
and at five,
            back out it goes.
People
        walk around
                    deaf and dumb

from the din,
        the gnashing
                of machinery.
And they only slow down
                chewing their gum
to blurt out:
        "Make money?"
A mommy
        offers
                her breast to her child.
The child,
        snot dripping from his nose,
suckles
    as if
        it's a dollar, not a breast—
he's tied up
        with some serious
                business.
Refresh yourself,
        if you're done for the day—
there's a constant
        electrical breeze.
If you want to go underground,
                just take the subway;
for the sky,
        take the elevated train.
The wagons
      go up
        as high as the smog,
and hang out
        around the heels
                of the buildings;

they drag
        their tails
                over the Brooklyn Bridge
and hide
        in their burrows
                beneath the Hudson.
You're blinded,
            you're dazzled,
but
    like a drumroll it raps
on your skull
        from the dark:
                "Maxwell House coffee:
Good
      to the last drop."
When the streetlamps
             are turned on
                to uproot the night,
I'll tell you,
        that's what I call light!
You look to your left,
           and holy moly!
Then to your right,
        moly holy!
Our boys in Moscow would do well to take notes.
And you can't
        see it all in one day!
That's New York for you.
              That's Broadway.
So tell me, now: how do you do?!
I'm delighted
        by New York as a city.

But I won't
              doff my cap
                          in awe.
We Soviets,
              after all,
                          have our pride:
we look down our noses
                          at the bourgeois.

August 6, 1925, New York

Let it out, Coolidge,
a shout of joy for the bridge!
For something this good,
                    I too won't grudge words.
Blush
      from my praise
                    like our flag's red material,
even if you are
                    the United States
                                        of
America.
The way
      a crazed believer
                              steps into a church,
or retreats
              to his cloister,
                              austere and rigid—
so I,
      in the evening's
                        graying mesmer,
set foot
        humbly on the Brooklyn Bridge.
The way a conqueror
                        advances on
                                    a shattered city
astride cannons whose muzzles
                                could swallow a giraffe—
so I, drunk off glory,
                        to live life with gusto,

clamber
            proudly
                        onto the Brooklyn Bridge.
The way a stupid artist
                        thrusts his eyes
into a museum Madonna,
                        in love and sharp-edged,
so I,
        from my perch
                    in the star-littered skies,
look out
        at New York
                        through the Brooklyn Bridge.
New York,
            which till evening
                        was stifling and grave,
has forgotten
            all about
                    its hardships and height,
and only
            the household spirits
rise up
        in the windows' transparent light.
From here
            the buzz of the elevated train
                            is barely audible.
And only
        that
                faint buzzing
lets you know—
                the trains
                        are rattling as they crawl,
as if someone
            were stacking dishes in a cupboard.

As a shopkeeper
                    starts
                            to ferry in
sugar
        from a mill
                    at the water's edge,
the ship masts
                    passing below the bridge
appear
        no bigger than safety pins.
I take great pride
                    in this
                            steel mile—
here my visions
                    arose in the flesh, made real;
here's a fight
                for construction
                                instead of just style,
a stern reckoning
                    of bolts
                            and steel.
If
    the world
                should come to an end,
and chaos
            tear
                the planet to shreds,
if this
        bridge
                alone should stand,
reared up
            over the dust of the dead—

then,
      just as from bone slivers
                        finer than needles,
huge lizards
            fatten up
                  to stand in museums,
so,
   with this bridge,
                  a centennial geologist
will be able
            to reconstruct
                        the present day.
"Imagine,
            this same steel paw,"
                        he'll attest,
"once connected
            the seas to the prairie;
from this very spot
                  Europe
                        burst into the West,
scattering
            Indian feathers
                        to the winds.
This rib here
            reminds one
                        of some giant machine—
just think,
            would its hands be able to reach,
with its steel foot
            planted firmly
                        on Manhattan,
to grab hold
            of the lip
                  of Brooklyn?

Judging from the wires
                    in this electrical braid,
I'd say
        this is the epoch
                    after the steam age—
these
    people
            had already
                    bawled out over the radio,
these
    people
            had already
                    taken off in airplanes.
Life
    here
        for some
                was a carefree joy,
and for others—
                a drawn-out
                        howl of hunger.
From this very spot
                the unemployed
threw themselves
                headfirst
                    into the Hudson.
From here on
            my picture develops
                        without a hitch,
to the feet of the stars
                along the string-cables.
I see—
        Mayakovsky
                stood on this bridge,

building
        his lines
                syllable by syllable.
I watch
        just as an Eskimo gapes at a train,
I dig in
        the way a tick latches onto your ear.
The Brooklyn Bridge—
yes indeed . . .
              It's one hell of a thing!"

1925

TO SERGEI YESENIN

As they say,
> to the other world
>> you've crossed over.

You're hurtling
> through the void,
>> ramming into stars.

No more royalties for you,
> no more bars.

Finally sober.

No, Yesenin,
> I'm
>> not joking.

The lump in my throat
> is grief,
>> not laughter.

I see you there,
> with your wrists slit open,

swinging
> your very own
>> bag of bones.

Come off it!
> Give it up!
>> Have you lost your mind?

Letting
> your cheeks
>> go pale
>>> with the chalk of death?!

You
> who could let loose
>> such streams of words,

like no one else
                      could
                                on earth.
We're crushed, we're at a loss.
                                Why'd you do it?
                                                What for?
The critics mutter:
                      "The blame here
falls on this
              and that . . .
                              Above all,
                                          on a lack of rapport,
which resulted
                in too much wine and beer."
If you'd swapped
                  your bohemians
                                    for the working class,
                                                            they say,
under their influence,
                        you'd have quit your brawling ways.
But what
          does the working class drink?
                                          Lemonade?
The working class too
                        is full of drunks.
If only
        you'd been assigned
                              to some union guy, they say,
you would
          have been so much better
                                      in terms of content.

You'd have written
                    a hundred
                                    lines
                                    a day,
like Doronin—
                endless
                        and tiresome nonsense.
The way I see it,
                    if they'd had
                                    their crazy way,
you probably would have
                            checked out even earlier.
Better to die
                from vodka
than from boredom!
Neither the noose
                    nor the little penknife
will reveal
            to us
                    the reasons for this waste.
Perhaps
        if there had been ink
                                in the Angleterre that night,
you'd have had
                no reason
                            to open your veins.
Your imitators were thrilled:
                                how about an encore!
A veritable platoon of them
                                have now done themselves in.
Why
    increase the number
                            of suicides?

Better
        to increase
                the production of ink!
Your tongue
        is now locked
                behind your teeth
                        for good.
Now
    is no time
            to be cultivating mysteries.
The people,
            language's creator,
have lost
        their clear-voiced
                    debauchee-apprentice.
And they come
                bearing scraps of requiem verse,
barely amended,
            from some prior
                    funeral.
Driving
        stupid rhymes
                uphill with a stick—
is that really
        how a poet
                should be remembered?
Your
    monument hasn't even been cast yet—
where is it,
            the buzz of bronze
                    or granite's granulations?—
but they've already
                delivered
                    to memory's latticework

the trash of reminiscences
                    and dedications.
Your name
            is sniveled into hankies,
your words
            are slobbered by Sobinov,
who croons
            beneath a scrawny birch:
"Not a word,
            oh my friend,
                    not a s-i-i-i-gh."
Eh,
    I'd sure like a word alone
with that what's-his-name,
                    with that Lohengrin!
Oh, to stand up
                and make a loud scene:
"I won't let you
            mumble and crumple
                        his verse!"
To deafen
            them all
                with a three-fingered whistle,
to send their grannies
                and goddamn mothers a curse!
To scatter all these
                talentless hacks to hell,
fanning
        the dark sails
                of their dinner jackets;
to make Kogan
            run for his life
                        pell-mell,

maiming
        passersby
                with the blades of his mustache.
The garbage
        shows no sign of letting up,
                        so far.
There's so much to do—
            we've got to keep up the pace.
We have
        to remake life,
                for a start;
then once we've remade it
                we can sing hymns of praise.
Our time
        is a tough one
                to write about,
but tell me,
        please,
                all you cripples:
what great man, anywhere,
                    ever
                        has picked out
a path
        because it was well-traveled
                    and simple?
The word
        is commander
                of the human army.
Forward march!
            Let time
                burst behind us
                    like bombs in the air.

Let the wind
            blowing back
                        to the old days carry
nothing
        but a clump of our hair.
For festivities
            our planet
                        is poorly designed.
We have
        to rip
            our joy
                        out of the days to come.
In this life
        to die
                is not so hard.
To make a life
            is significantly harder.

1926

Citizen taxman!
               Please forgive the imposition.
Why thank you,
             don't trouble yourself . . .
                                   I'll stand.
I'm here to discuss
             a rather
                   delicate issue:
the poet's
         proper place
               in the workforce.
In line
      with all those who own
                   granaries and land,
I too am subject
           to taxation and penalty.
Five hundred per half-year
                 is what
                   you demand,
plus twenty-five more
             for failure to declare.
My labor
       is akin
           to any
              other.
Take a look—
            you'll see just what I've lost;
all my
      expenses
             incurred in production,

and just how much
                    my raw materials cost.
You're familiar,
            of course,
                        with the concept of rhyme.
Let's say
        some line
                ends with the word
                                "dad"—
why then,
            repeating the syllables
                            in a following line,
we put in
        some sort of
                rat-a-tat-tad.
In your terms,
                rhyme
                is a bill of exchange.
Pay in full at line's end!—
                        that's the intention.
So you sift
            through suffixes and inflections—
                                small change
in your dwindling cash box
                    of conjugations
                            and declensions.
You start trying
            to stuff some word
                        into your line,
but it won't fit—
                it breaks if you force it.
Citizen taxman,
            I'll tell you no lie—

words
        cost your poet a fortune.
In our terms,
             rhyme
                  is a keg—
a powder keg.
              Its fuse
                  is the line.
The line burns down,
                the line goes bang!
and as a stanza
            the whole city
                  is sent flying.
Where can you find them,
                and at what price—
knock-'em-dead rhymes
                that won't ever fail you?
Maybe
        some half-dozen
                original rhymes
still exist somewhere
              in Venezuela.
And I yearn
            to rush off—
                  somewhere cold, somewhere hot.
I set out,
            tangled up in advances and loans.
Citizen,
            take my travel expenses into account!
Poetry—
          all of it!—
                is a journey into the unknown.
Poetry
        is like mining for radium.

Every gram mined
                    takes a year of labor.
For the sake
          of a single word
                          you expend
thousands of tons
                of crude verbal ore.
But how
        incineratingly
                      those single words burn
compared
        to the decay
                    of their unrefined peers!
Those single words
                  have the power to move
millions of hearts
                over thousands of years.
Of course,
          there are various sorts of poet.
So many
        have the magic touch!
Like a conjuror,
                they'll pull a line
                                  out of their throat
or even out of someone else's,
                              in a pinch.
What can I say
              about the lyrical castrati?!
They'll steal
            a stranger's line
                            with a smile on their face.
It's just
        your typical
                    embezzlement and robbery—

quite a bit of that plaguing our country these days.
All
    of today's
                odes and verses,
belted out loud
                in rounds of applause,
will enter
            history
                as the overhead expenses
for what
        we've done—
                        just two or three of us.
You'll go through
                    forty pounds of salt, I've heard,
and smoke
            a hundred cigarettes,
before
        you extract
                    one precious word
from the artesian
                human depths.
Well, that right there
                        should lower
                                    my rates.
Knock
        the wheel of a zero
                        off my tax!
One ruble ninety kopecks
                        for a hundred cigarettes,
one sixty for table salt!
Your form
            has question after question:
"Any trips abroad?
                    Yes or no?"

But what
        if I've taken
                a dozen Pegasuses
out for a ride
        over the past
                fifteen years?!
Sir, please try
        to understand my situation;
In this corner you ask
                about assets
                        and servants.
But what
        if I am
                a leader of the nation,
and at the same time
                in the nation's service?
The working class
                speaks
                        through our words,
and we,
        the proletariat,
                        are the engine moving the pen.
Over the years
                the machine
                        of the soul gets worn out.
They say:
        "To the archive with him,
                        no more writing,
                                he's done!"
To love and to dare,
                there's less and less inclination,
and time
        gets a running start
                and smashes my head.

We come
           to the most horrible of depreciations—
the depreciation
                of the heart and the soul.
And when
         that sun,
                  like some fattened-up hog,
rises
     over a future
                without beggars or cripples,
then
     I'll
         rot,
             dead in a ditch
alongside
         a dozen colleagues—
                             my people.
Tally up
        my
           posthumous dues!
I contend—
          and I know this is true—
that among
          all of today's
                        dealers and tricksters,
I alone
       will be stuck
                    in unfathomable debt.
To blare
        like a brass-throated siren
                                 is our pledge,
in the fog of philistinism,
                           at the heart of the tempest.

The poet
            is always
                        in the universe's debt,
paying out
            , exorbitant
                        fines
                                    and interest.
I
  am in debt
            to Broadway's dazzling streetlamps,
to you,
        the Bagdadi sky,
to the Red Army,
                    to the cherry trees of Japan—
to everything
                about which
                            I haven't yet written.
But anyway,
            what's the point
                        of all this debt collection?
Just to take aim with rhyme
                        and let rhythm go berserk?
No—the poet's word
                        is your resurrection,
your immortality,
                    mister government clerk.
Centuries from now
                    you can pick out a line
from its paper box
                    and turn back time!
And the day
            of the taxman
                        will dawn again

with its stinking ink
                    and miraculous shine.
Self-assured denizen of the present day,
Book a ticket
            to immortality
                        at the NKPS,
and, calculating
            the effect of my verse,
                        prorate
my earnings
        over three hundred years!
But the strength of a poet
                    isn't just to give
posterity
        the hiccups
                as they read about you.
No!
    Nowadays also
                the poet's rhyme lives
as a caress,
            a slogan,
                a bayonet,
                    a knout.
Citizen taxman,
                I tell you what:
I'll cross off
            all these zeroes
                        and just pay you five!
I'm within my rights
                to demand
                        a spot
in the ranks
        of the poorest
                    workers and peasants alive.

And if
        you think
                    that all I do
is help myself
                    to the verbiage of somebody else,
well then,
            comrades,
                        this pen's for you—
you can
        give it a try
                    yourselves!

1926

In a kiss, whether on the hands
                         or the lips,
in the trembling of a body
                         of those close to me,
the red
        color
              of my Republics
also
     should
            blaze bright.
I have no love
              for Parisian love:
dress any old female
                    up in silks,
and stretching out, I'll doze off,
                              having said
                                         "down, boy"
to the dogs
           of animal passion.
You alone are my
                equal in size;
stand, then, beside me,
                       eyebrow to eyebrow,
let me
       tell of this
                    important evening
in normal
          human fashion.
It's five o'clock,
                  and now

the dense forest
                of people
                        has settled down.
The populated city
                is deserted,
and I hear only
                the whistling argument
of trains to Barcelona.
In the black sky,
                lightning's tread,
the thunder
        of swearwords
                        in a celestial drama—
this is no storm,
                but
                        simply
jealousy
        moving mountains.
Don't believe the raw materials
                        of stupid words,
don't be afraid
                of that trembling—
I will bridle,
                I will subdue
the feelings
        of scions of the nobility.
The measles of my passion
                        may come off in scabs,
but my joy
        is inexhaustible;
of it, simply
                and at length,
I will speak in verse.

Jealousy,
        wives,
                tears . . .
                        to hell with them!—
my eyelids will swell,
                might as well be the Viy.
It's not just about me—
                        I
                        am jealous
on behalf of Soviet Russia.
I've seen
        the patches on your shoulders,
consumption
        licks them
                with its breath.
But you see,
        it's not our fault—
one hundred million
                were in a bad way.

Now
    we are
        gentler with such types—
you won't straighten out very many
                        with sports—
but we in Moscow
                need you too—
we don't have enough
                long-legged girls.
It's not for you,
        through snows
                        and typhus
having marched
        upon those legs,

to give them up
                here
                        for caresses
at dinners
        with oil magnates.

Don't think about it,
                        squinting your eyes
beneath their straightened arches.
Just come here,
                come to the crossroads
of my big
        and awkward arms.
You don't want to?
                Then stay and spend the winter,
and this
        insult
                we'll add to the general bill.
All the same,
                someday
                        I'll come and take you—
you alone
        or along with Paris.

1928

I'd gnaw out
        bureaucracy's heart
                like a wolf.
Not a bit of respect
        for mandates.
Send every
        piece of paper
                straight to hell
along with its mother.
                But not this one . . .
Along the long front
        of cabins
            and coupés
the courteous
        clerk
           makes his way.
They're handing in passports,
            and I too
                must hand over
my booklet
        in its crimson cover.
Some passports
        are greeted with a smile
while others
        are treated like trifles.
With deference,
        for example,
            they collect passports
bearing the double-sleeper
        English lion.

Eyeing
      the good fellow from bottom to top,
never ceasing
         to bow,
they collect
        as if accepting a tip
the passport
         of an American.
At a Pole's
       they stare
           like a goat at a billboard.
At a Pole's
       they goggle their eyes
like awkward
         police-elephants:
where'd this come from,
            and what are these
geographical novelties?
And without turning
          their cabbage heads,
without
     a hint
        of emotion,
without
     blinking an eye,
          they take passports from Danes
and other
      assorted
        Swedes.
And suddenly,
      it's as though
          he's been scalded:
the kind sir's face
      is distorted.

The government
              clerk
                       has just taken hold
of my
       red-skinned giant of a passport.
He holds it
            like a bomb
                          or a porcupine,
or like a double-edged
                         razor blade;
he holds it
            like
                a twenty-fanged
snake
      of six-foot size.
The porter's eye
                 gives a meaningful
                                     wink,
at least
         he'll carry my things for free.
The gendarme
              looks questioningly
                                   at the detective;
the detective,
               right back at the gendarme.
Oh, with what pleasure
                         by the gendarmerie
I would be
           flogged and crucified,
for having
           in my hands
                        such a hammery,

sickle-faced
                Soviet
                        passport.
I'd gnaw out
                bureaucracy's heart
                                like a wolf.
Not a bit of respect
                for mandates.
Send every
                piece of paper
                                straight to hell
along with its mother.
                        But not this one . . .

I
  pull it out
                from my wide trouser legs,
a duplicate
                of precious cargo.
Read it
        and envy me—
                        I
                        am a citizen
of the Soviet Union.

1929

First Introduction to a Long Poem

Most esteemed
                comrades of posterity!
Rummaging
            through the present day's
                            petrified shit,
studying the darkness of our era,
you
    may also
            want to know about me.
And one of your scholars
                    may just impart,
countering the swarm of questions
                            with his erudition,
that indeed there lived
                    a certain boiled-water bard,
standing up to raw water
                    in fierce opposition.
Professor,
        you can take off the bicycle of your glasses!
I'll tell the story
            of my time
                    and myself.
I, a latrine-cleaner
                and water boy,
by the revolution
            called up and deployed,
set off for the front
                from the lordly flower beds

of poetry,
             the capricious wench.
Her garden sown so prettily,
the daughter,
             dacha,
                    pond,
                          and peace—
"I planted it, so by your leave
I'll water it too, if you please."
Some pour verse from watering cans,
some just spit it
                  from their mouths—
curly-headed Mitreikins,
                         levelheaded Kudreikins—
who the hell can sort them out!
We can't stop this with a quarantine—
they'll mandolin beneath the walls:
"Tara-tina, tara-tina,
Trrrrrills . . ."
It's not much of an honor
                          that compared to such roses
my creations shot up like towering edifices
over public squares
                    hacking up tuberculosis,
·crawling with whores, hoodlums,
                                  and syphilis.
I'm
    sick and tired
                   of agitprop, too;
I too
      would rather scribble
                             more romances for you—
there's more money in them,
                             as well as more charm.

But I
        chose
                to subdue
                        myself,
standing on the throat
                        of my song.
Comrades of posterity,
                        listen to me,
an agitator,
                a loudmouth ringleader.
Drowning out
                poetry's mellifluous streams,
I'll step across
                dainty volumes of lyrics,
like a real live person
                        speaking with living peers.
I'll come to you
                in the far communist future,
but not
        like some Yeseninized folk-hero crooner.
My verse will reach you
                        over the crests of ages
and over the heads
                of poets and states.
My verse will reach you,
                        but not like this:
not like an arrow
                from some cupid's hunting-lyre,
not like a worn-down nickel
                        reaches a numismatist,
and not like light from a dead star.
My verse
        will smash its way
                        through the years' bulk

and arrive—
                tangible,
                        ponderous,
                                crude,
the way, in our time,
                the aqueduct
built by Roman slaves
                appeared.
In the funeral mounds of books
                        where verse lies buried,
if you should discover my lines' iron shards,
run
    your hands over them,
                        but be wary
as you would of an old weapon
                        still dangerously sharp.
I'm
    not one
        to caress the ear
                with words;
no virginal ear
                ringed in soft curls
will burn red,
                assaulted by some piece of semi-smut.
With the troops of my pages
                        in parade unfurled,
I tour and inspect
                my lines' formidable front.
The verses stand at attention,
                        heavy as lead,
ready for death
                and for glory immortal.
The long poems are rigid and still,
                        having leveled

muzzle to muzzle
                    their gaping titles.
The favorites
          among all the armed forces'
                              troops,
the cavalry of witticisms
                    is frozen there,
in position, poised
                to charge with a whoop,
sharp lances
          of rhymes raised in the air.
And all these troops,
                    armed to the teeth and beyond,
that have flown by
                for twenty victorious years,
to the very last page,
                    all I've got
I give to you,
          the planet's proletariat.
Any enemy
          of the working class en masse
is my enemy too,
                sworn
                    and ancient.
We were ordered
                to march
                    under the red flag
by years of toil
                and days of malnourishment.
We opened up
                every volume
                    of Marx

like opening
            the shutters
                        in our own home,
but we didn't have to read
                        to understand
on which side we belonged,
                        in whose camp.
We
    learned about the dialectic,
                        but not from Hegel.
It dug into our verse
                in the roar of battles,
when
        under our gunfire
                        the bourgooeys turned tail
and ran
        just as we
                had once run from them.
Lagging
        behind genius
                        like an inconsolable widow,
let fame
        trudge along in a funeral procession—
die then, my verse,
                but die like a soldier,
like our nameless
                masses, on the offensive!
I don't give a damn
                about megapoundage of bronze,
I don't give a damn
                about marble slime.
We'll divvy up the glory—
                we're all friends here.

Let our true
            shared monument
be the socialism
            we've built
                        under fire.
Posterity,
            consult your dictionaries' flotsam:
from Lethe
            will emerge
                        the remains of such words as
"prostitution,"
            "blockade," ·
                        "tuberculosis."
For you
            who are healthy
                        and never at a loss,
the poet
            licked up
                        consumption's spit-wads
with the raspy tongue of his posters.
I'm starting to resemble,
                        with my tail of years,
those monstrous
            fossil-dinosaurs.
Comrade Life,
            let's
                        get up to speed—
let's live
            what's left of our days
                        by the FYP.
My lines
            haven't left me with a ruble
                        of savings,

cabinetmakers
                    haven't done up my rooms
                                        in mahogany.
And besides
            a freshly washed shirt,
there's nothing I need,
                    I say in all honesty.
Appearing
            before the C C C
                        of future
                                    sunny days,
over the heads
            of poetry's
                        money-grubbers and skinflints,
by way of a party membership card
                        I'll raise
all the hundred volumes
                    of my
                            partisan booklets.

December 1929–January 1930

1

She loves me? She loves me not? I wring my hands
breaking off fingers
                          and scattering them
the way people tear petals
                                  off daisy chains
and release them to May's winds in a guessing game
let scissors and razor reveal my gray hairs
Let the silver of my amassed years ring out
I hope and believe it will never come
to me, your shameful common sense

4

It's after one, you must be in bed
The Milky Way runs like a silver Oka through the night
I'm in no rush and I see no need
to wake or worry you with lightning telegrams
as they say, the case is closed
the love boat has smashed against convention
You and I are quits and there's no point in listing
mutual hurts misfortunes and offenses
Just look what quiet fills the world
Night slapped the sky with a heavy tax of stars
at times like this you stand up and speak
to the ages to history and to the universe

1928–1930

To Everyone

Don't blame anyone for my death, and please don't gossip. The deceased really hated that.

Mama, sisters, and comrades forgive me—this isn't a solution (I don't recommend it to others) but for me there's no other way out.

Lily—love me.

Comrade Government my family is Lily Brik, Mama, my sisters, and Veronika Vitoldovna Polonskaya.

If you can provide a decent life for them—thanks.

Give the poems I've started to the Briks they'll sort them out.

As they say—

"the case is cloved"

The love boat

has smashed against convention.

Life and I are quits

and there's no point in listing

mutual hurts

misfortunes

and offenses.

Best of luck to those I leave behind

Vladimir

Mayakovsky

April 12, 1930

Comrades at RAPP

don't think me cowardly

Seriously—it can't be helped.

Greetings.

Tell Yermilov it's too bad he took down the slogan we should have fought it out.

VM

Use the 2,000 rub. in my desk drawer to pay my taxes. You can get the rest from the State Publishing House

V. M.

Selected Long Poems

A Tetraptych

Your thought,
daydreaming in a brain gone soft,
like some fattened-up lackey on a grease-stained couch,
I'll tease against the bloodied shreds of my heart;
I'll jeer all I want, insolent and caustic.

There isn't a single gray hair in my soul,
nor any geriatric tenderness!
Thundering the world with the might of my voice,
I go forth, gorgeous,
twenty-two years old.

Tender people!
You play your love on violins.
The brute bangs his out on kettledrums.
But you can't turn yourselves inside out, like I can,
to be pure lips and nothing else!

Come, one and all, and be taught—
you there, out of the drawing room, batiste-woman,
you decorous bureaucrat of the angelic league.
And another, you there, leafing calmly through lips
like a chef through the pages of a cookbook.

If you want,
I'll be rabid, crazy for flesh,
and then—like the sky changing tint—
if you like,

I'll be irreproachably tender,
not a man, but a cloud in pants!

I don't believe in any flowery Nice!
Through my lips a hymn will rise again
to men laid up like a hospital
and women worn out like a proverb.

1

You think these are the ravings of malaria?

This happened;
it happened in Odessa.

"I'll be there at four," said Maria.

Eight.
Nine.
Ten.

And at this point, the evening,
sullen,
decembry,
slipped away from the windows
into wretched night.

Into my decrepit back the candelabras
guffawed and neighed.

You wouldn't even recognize me now:
I'm a hulk of sinews,
squirming
and moaning.

What on earth could such a glob desire?
But in fact, the glob desires quite a lot!

After all, it doesn't matter to you
if you're bronzed,
if your heart's like a cold piece of iron.
At night you still want to hide your clangor
in something soft,
something female.

And so,
enormous,
I stoop at the window,
melting the glass with my forehead.
Will there be love or will there not?
And what kind—
big or teensy-weensy?
It couldn't be big, with a body like that:
it must be a small,
meek little lovelet.
It shies away from automobile horns.
Likes the bells on horse-drawn buggies.

Again and again,
staring into the rain,
my face to its pockmarked face,
I wait,
splashed by the thunder of the city's breakers.

Midnight, running around with a knife,
finally caught what it was chasing
and slashed away—
"be gone!"

Twelve o'clock fell
like a convict's head from the scaffold.

In the windowpanes, gray droplets of rain
howl together as one,
piling up into a grimace,
as if it were chimeras howling
from Notre Dame in Paris.

Cursed woman!
What, you haven't had enough?
Soon a cry will tear my mouth to shreds.

Then I hear:
quietly,
like a sick man from his bed,
a nerve jumps down to the floor.
At first
it simply goes for a stroll,
barely, barely moving;
then it breaks into a run,
agitated,
distinct.
Soon the nerve and two more like it
are rushing about in a desperate dance!

On the bottom floor, the plaster comes crashing down.

Nerves—
big ones,
little ones,
so many!—
gallop around in a fury

until soon
the nerves' little legs give out!

But night keeps on sliming and sliming through the room—
the eye, grown heavy, can't rise out of the slime.

The doors suddenly clattered
as if the hotel's
teeth were chattering.

You walked in,
brusque as "take that!"
torturing the suede of your glove,
and said:
"You know what?
I'm getting married."

By all means, go ahead.
It doesn't matter.
I'll be strong.
See how calm I am!
Like a dead man's
pulse.

Remember
the way you used to talk?
"Jack London,
money,
love,
passion."
But I saw only one thing:
you were a Gioconda
who needed to be stolen!

And you were stolen.

Once more I'll play the game of love,
fire illuminating the bend of my brows.
What of it!
Even in a burnt-out house,
sometimes homeless tramps will take shelter!

Are you teasing?
"There are fewer emeralds of madness in you
than a beggar has kopecks."
Remember!
Pompeii perished
when people started teasing Vesuvius!

Hey!
Gentlemen!
Fans
of sacrilege,
crimes,
and carnage!
Have you, by chance,
seen the most terrifying thing of all—
my face
when
I
am absolutely calm?

And I feel it—
"I"
is too small for me.
Someone inside is trying hard to break free.

Hello!
Who's speaking?
Mama?
Mama!
Your son is beautifully ill!
Mama!
His heart is on fire.
Tell his sisters, Lyuda and Olya,
there's no place left for him to go.
Every word,
every joke
he spews from his scorching mouth,
leaps like a naked prostitute
from a burning brothel.

The people catch a whiff—
it smells like burnt flesh!
They've gathered some men.
All shiny!
In helmets!
But hey, no boots allowed!
Inform the firemen:
you climb up to a burning heart with caresses.
I can handle this myself.
I'll draw a few barrels of tears from my eyes.
If I can just brace myself against my ribs,
I'll jump out! Jump! Jump! Jump!
I collapsed.
You can't jump out of your heart!

From the cracked-open lips
of my scorching face,
the charred cinder of a kiss is ready to leap.

Mama!
I can't sing.
The choir loft in the chapel of my heart is occupied!

Scorched little figures of words and numbers
stream from my skull
like children from a burning building.
In the same way, fear,
trying to grab hold of the sky,
raised high
the burning hands of the *Lusitania*.

Into the quietness
of people trembling in their apartments,
a hundred-eyed glow is bursting from the docks.
O final cry—
you, at least,
moan out to the centuries that I'm on fire!

2

Glorify me!
The great are no match for me.
Over everything that's been done
I stamp *nihil*.

I never
want to read anything.
Books?
What good are books!

I used to think
books were made as follows:
a poet shows up,

effortlessly unclenches his lips,
and at once the inspired simpleton sings out—
come and get it!
But as it turns out,
before the singing can start,
they pace to and fro, feet callused from wandering,
and the dim-witted minnow of imagination
quietly wallows in the slime of the heart.
And all the while, as they strum their rhymes,
boiling up a broth of loves and nightingales,
the tongueless street writhes—
it has no way to cry out or to converse.

Having grown prideful, once more we raise
the cities' towers of Babel,
but God
razes
the cities into pastures,
confounding our words.

The street bore its torment in silence.
A cry stood still and erect in its gullet.
Chubby taxis and bony horse-cabs
bristled, stuck in its craw.
Its breast is all pedestrianed out,
stomped flatter than consumption.

The city locked the road up in gloom.

And when—
all the same!—
the street hawked a crowd up onto the square,
casting aside the portico parked on its throat,
it seemed

God, like someone who had been robbed, went on the warpath
in the choirs of the archangels' chorale!

But the street just plopped down and belted out:
"Let's get something to eat!"

Krupps and little Kruppikins paint the city's face
with a furrow of menacing brows,
while in its mouth,
the little corpselets of dead words decay;
only two still live, getting fatter—
"scum"
and another one,
apparently "borscht."

Poets,
sodden with wailing and sobs,
rush away from the street, tousling their mops:
"How can we sing, using just those two words,
the lady,
the love,
and the wee flower wet with dew?"

On the poets' heels
are the street's thousands:
students,
prostitutes,
contractors.

Gentlemen!
Stop right there!
You're not beggars,
don't you dare ask for spare change!

We, the robust ones,
with a six-foot stride,
shouldn't listen to them, but just tear them to shreds—
those
who've attached themselves like some free magazine
    supplement
to every double bed!

Are we supposed to ask them humbly:
"Help me!"—
to pray for a hymn
or some oratory?!
We ourselves are creators in a burning hymn—
the noise of the factory and the laboratory.

What do I care for Faust
on his fairy-tale rockets
sliding with Mephistopheles across the heavenly parquet!
I know it well:
the nail lodged in my boot
is more of a nightmare than all Goethe's fantasy!

I,
the most golden-mouthed of them all,
whose every word
rebirths the soul
and throws the body a name-day bash,
say unto you:
the tiniest dust-speck of life
is worth more than all I've ever done or will do!

Listen up!
The present day's shoutlipped Zarathustra
is preaching

as he runs around and moans!
We,
with a face like a slept-on sheet,
with lips that sag like a chandelier,
we,
the inmates of the leprosarium city,
where gold and filth have given leprosy ulcers—
we are cleaner than any Venetian azure
washed by seas and suns at once!

I don't give a damn
that Homers and Ovids
didn't have anyone like us,
pockmarked with soot.
I know—
the sun itself would go dim
if it could see the deposits of gold in our souls!

Sinews and muscles are more reliable than prayers.
As if we would beg for time's mercy!
We—
every one of us—
hold in our five fingers
the drive-belts of worlds!

This is what led to my Golgothas on the stages
of Petrograd, Moscow, Odessa, and Kiev,
and there wasn't a single person
who
wouldn't have cried:
"Crucify,
crucify him!"
But to me,
people—

even those who have hurt me—
are nearer and dearer than anything.

Have you ever seen
a dog lick the hand that beats it?!

I,
laughed at by the present-day tribe,
like some long,
dirty joke,
see someone approaching across mountains of time,
someone no one else sees.

Where men's meager vision falls short,
out there, leading the hungry hordes,
wearing a thorny crown of revolutions,
the year '16 draws nigh.

And for you, I shall be its precursor;
I am everywhere there is pain;
in every drop of the current of tears,
I've nailed myself to the cross.
Nothing can be forgiven anymore.
I've burnt out every soul where tenderness was nourished.
That was harder than storming
a thousand thousand Bastilles!

And when,
proclaiming through revolt
his coming,
you step out to meet your savior,
for you
I'll tear out my soul
and stomp on it—

to make it nice and big!—
and give it to you all bloodied, for a banner.

3

Ach, what's the point,
where's all this coming from,
this brandishing of dirty fists
in the bright sunny fun!

A thought of madhouses
arrived
and drew a curtain of despair across the head.

And—
just like, when a dreadnought goes down,
men escape the choking spasms
by diving out of a hatch—
so Burliuk, driven mad, clambered out
through his own
screaming-wide-open eye.
Having almost bloodied his cried-out eyelids,
he crawled out,
got up,
took a few steps
and, with a tenderness you wouldn't expect from such a fat
    man,
abruptly announced:
"Very good!"

It is indeed very good when your soul's wrapped up,
safe from prying eyes, in a yellow blouse.
It's very good,

when you're cast into the teeth of the scaffold,
to cry out:
"Drink Van Houten's cocoa!"

And that second,
sparkling like a Bengal light,
loud,
I would not trade for anything,
no, not for any . . .

But out of the cigar smoke
like a liqueur glass
stretched the drink-sodden face of Severyanin.

How dare you call yourself a poet
and, done up all pretty in gray, twitter like a quail!
These days
we need
to carve our way with brass knuckles
into the world's skull!

You
who are troubled by one thought alone—
"how elegant is my dancing?"—
see how I amuse
myself—
a town-square
cardsharp and pimp!

On you
who are sodden with your own enamoredness,
from whom
a tear has poured through the ages,
I'll turn my back

and place the sun like a monocle
into my gaping eye.

Arrayed in unbelievable finery,
I'll walk the earth
aiming to please and to burn,
with Napoleon out in front
like a pug on my leash.

The earth will lie down on its back like a woman,
its fleshes all fidgety, wanting to give themselves up;
things will come to life—
the things' lips
will lisp out:
"Bobble, bobble, bobble!"

Suddenly
the clouds
and various other cloudy stuff
launched an incredible rumpus up there,
as if it were workers in white dispersing,
having declared against the sky an embittered strike.

Thunder, in a rage, clambered out from behind a cloud,
cleared his enormous nostrils in provocation,
and for a second the sky's face was contorted
into the stern grimace of the iron von Bismarck.

And someone
tangled up in cloudy fetters
stretched his hands out toward a café—
and it seemed somehow feminine,
somehow tender,
and yet also like the carriage of a cannon.

You think
it was the sun, with the utmost tenderness
patting that café on the cheek?
No! It's General Galliffet approaching once more
to send the rebels to the firing squad!

You on the streets: hands out of your pockets—
pick up a stone, a knife, or a bomb,
and if there's someone without any hands,
let him come too and fight with his forehead!

Come, my little hungry ones,
sweaty ones,
meek ones,
you who have gone sour in flea-ridden filth!

Come forward!
Mondays and Tuesdays
we'll repaint with blood into holidays!
Let the earth remember under our knives
whom she tried to debase!
The same earth
that's grown fat like a lover
after some Rothschild is done with her!

Let flags flutter in a feverish fusillade,
like for any other upstanding holiday—
lift up higher, you streetlamp posts,
the bloodied carcasses of grain merchants.

I've cursed myself hoarse,
begged and pleaded,
cut throats,

snuck up behind someone
to gnaw into his flanks.

In the sky, red as the Marseillaise,
the dying sunset shuddered.

This is sheer madness.

None of this will happen.

Night will come,
take a bite,
and eat you up.

Do you see—
the sky is again playing Judas
with a handful of betrayal-spattered stars?

It's arrived.
It feasts like Mamai,
its ass parked on top of the city.
This night we'll never break through with our eyes,
black as the traitor Azef!

I shiver, flung into the corners of taverns,
I spill wine all over my soul and the tablecloth,
and I see:
in the corner—her eyes are round—
the Mother of God bores into my heart with her eyes.

Why would you, in this daubed-up cliché,
bestow your shine upon a tavern crowd!
Don't you see—once more

they prefer Barabbas
to your spat-upon Golgothite?

Perhaps it's by design that my face,
in the jumbled hash of humanity,
isn't any newer than anyone else's.
I,
perhaps,
am the most beautiful
of all your sons.

Grant to all those
who have grown moldy in joy
the swift death of time,
so that the children might grow up:
the little boys become fathers,
the little girls get pregnant.

And let all newborns be overgrown
with the inquisitive gray hair of the Magi,
and people will come
and baptize their children
with the names of my poems.

I, who sing the machine and England,
am, perhaps, nothing more
than the thirteenth apostle
in the most ordinary of Gospels.

And when my voice
hoots out obscenely—
hour to hour,
for days at a time,

perhaps it's Jesus Christ stopping to sniff
the forget-me-nots of my soul.

4

Maria! Maria! Maria!
Let me in, Maria!
I can't take it anymore out on the streets!
You don't want to?
You're waiting
till my cheeks cave in like a ditch,
and, nibbled at by everyone,
flavorless,
I arrive
and toothlessly mumble
that today I am
"surprisingly honest."

Maria,
you see—
I'm already stooping.

In the streets
people poke holes in the fat of their four-story goiters,
thrust their little eyes out,
rubbed down to nubbins over forty years;
they giggle themselves silly,
for in my teeth—
once again!—
is the stale bread of yesterday's caresses.

Rain has sobbed all over the sidewalk,
that puddled-up petty thief;
dripping wet, it licks the street's cobblestoned corpse,

and on its grizzled eyelashes—
yes!—
on its frosty icicle lashes
are tears from its eyes—
you guessed it!—
from the downcast eyes of its drainpipes.

While the rain's snout sucked on pedestrians,
in carriages, fat athlete after fat athlete gleamed:
the people burst open,
stuffed through and through,
and their lard oozed through the cracks;
the cud of old meat patties
together with slurped-down bread
streamed like a murky river from their carriages.

Maria!
How can I squeeze a quiet word into their fat-swollen ear?
A bird
begs for its living through song.
It sings,
hungry and clear-voiced;
but I am a man, Maria,
just a simple man,
hawked up by consumptive night into Presnya's dirty hand.

Maria, do you want such a man?
Let me in, Maria!
With a spasm of my fingers I'll wring the bell's iron neck!

Maria!

The streets' pastures are growing wild.
The crowd's fingers are like a sore on my neck.

Open up!

I'm in pain!

You see—pins
from ladies' hats are stuck in my eyes!

You let me in.

My child!
Do not be afraid
if on my bovine neck
a soggy mountain of sweaty-bellied women is perched—
it's just that I drag through life
a million enormous pure loves
and a million million dirty little lovelets.
Do not be afraid
that once more
in the foul weather of betrayal
I'll nuzzle up to thousands of pretty faces—
"lovers of Mayakovsky!"—
that's just the dynasty
of queens enthroned on the heart of a madman.

Maria, come closer!

Whether in undressed shamelessness
or fearful trembling,
yield to me your lips' ever-blooming charm:
my heart and I have never made it as far as May;
in the life I've lived so far
it's just one hundred Aprils.

Maria!
The poet sings songs to Tiana,
but I'm
made of meat,
entirely human—
I simply ask for your body
as Christians ask,
"Give us this day
our daily bread."

Maria—give it to me!

Maria!
I'm afraid I'll forget your name
the way a poet is afraid to forget
some word
born in nighttime torment,
equal in greatness to God.

Your body
I will care for and love
the way a soldier,
hacked to pieces by war,
useless,
belonging to no one,
cares for his one remaining leg.

Maria—
you don't want to?
You don't want to!

Ha!

In that case, once again,
dark and depressed,
I'll take my heart,
having dribbled it with tears,
and carry it with me
like a dog
carrying home
to kennel
its train-severed paw.

My heart's blood brightens up the road's day,
sticking like flowers to the dust on my jacket.
The sun, like Herodias, one thousand times
dances round the earth—
the Baptist's head.

And when my number of years
dances to its end,
a million bloodstains will pave the path
back to my father's house.

I'll clamber out,
filthy from nights spent in ditches,
and stand by his side;
I'll bend down
and speak into his ear:

"Listen up, Mister God!
Aren't you bored
with dipping your kind eyes
every day into the jelly of clouds?
Why don't we—you know what?—
set up a merry-go-round
around the tree of the knowledge of good and evil!

Omnipresent, you'll be in every cupboard,
and we'll set such wines out on the table
that even sullen Peter the Apostle
will want to get up and dance the Kickapoo.
And in paradise once again we'll plant little Eves:
just say the word,
and this very night, for you,
from every boulevard
I'll round up all the most beautiful girls.

Would you like that?

You wouldn't?

You're shaking your head, shaggy-hair?
Knitting your hoary eyebrows?
You think
that guy
behind you, with the wings,
knows what love is?

I too am an angel, or anyway, I was one—
I looked into your eyes like a sugar lamb,
but no more will I present to horses
the sculptured vases of my Sèvres-porcelain torment.
Almighty, you thought up a pair of hands
and made sure
everyone would have a head—
why didn't you think
to make it possible, without torment,
to kiss, and kiss, and kiss?!

I thought you were a big, omnipotent God,
but you're just a dropout, a minute little godlet.

See here? I'm bending down
and out of my boot
I'm fetching a little cobbler's knife.

You winged bastards!
Huddle up in heaven!
Ruffle your feathers in a terrified quake!
I'll cut you wide open—you, reeking of incense,
from here all the way to Alaska!

Let me in!

You can't stop me.
Wrong
or right,
I couldn't be calmer.
Look—
once again the stars are beheaded
and the sky is bloodied with carnage!

Hey, you!
Sky!
Take off your hat!
I'm walking here!

Nobody hears me.

The universe sleeps,
its paw curled under
an enormous ear riddled with stars for ticks.

1914–1915

Prologue

To all of you
I like or have liked,
kept safe by the icons in the cave of your soul,
like a goblet of wine in a festive toast,
I raise my skull, brimming with verse.

More and more often I think—
wouldn't it be better to place
the period of a bullet at my end?
Tonight,
just in case,
I'm giving a farewell concert.

Memory!
Assemble in the great hall of my brain
inexhaustible rows of beloveds.
Pour laughter from eye to eye.
Deck the night in bygone weddings.
Pour joy from body to body.
Let this night be forgotten by no one.
Tonight I will be playing the flute.
On my own backbone.

1

I crumple miles of streets with the sweep of my paces.
Where can I go, melting this hell!
In the mind of what divine Hoffmann
were you dreamt up, cursed woman?!

The streets are too narrow for this happy storm.
The holiday keeps ladling out well-dressed people.
I'm thinking.
Thoughts, clots of blood,
sick and coagulated, crawl out of my skull.

I,
the wonderworker of everything festive,
myself have no one with whom to attend the festival.
Right now I'll up and fall flat on my back
and bash out my brains on the stone of Nevsky!
I went and blasphemed.
Screamed that there is no God,
but God took such a woman from the depths of hell
that before her a mountain would get nervous and tremble;
he dragged her out and commanded:
love!

God is pleased.
On a steep slope beneath heaven,
a worn-out man went wild and died.
God rubs the palms of his little hands together.
God is thinking:
just you wait, Vladimir!
It was he, of course it was he—
to keep me from guessing who you really were—
who thought to give you a real husband
and to place human sheet music on your piano.
If I could suddenly steal up to your bedroom door,
and make the sign of the cross on the quilt above you,
I know—
the smell of burning fur would fill the air,
and the flesh of the devil would give out sulfurous smoke.

But instead, until early morning,
horrified that someone had taken you away to love,
I rushed around
and engraved my cries into verse lines,
a jeweler gone already half mad.
I should play some cards!
Rinse the throat
of my moaned-out heart with wine.

I don't need you!
Don't want you!
All the same
I know:
I'll soon kick the bucket.

If it's true that you exist,
God,
my God,
if the carpet of stars was woven by you,
if this pain,
daily multiplied,
is a torture sent down by you, O Lord,
then put on your judge's chain.
Await my visit.
I'm a punctual guy;
I won't delay a single day.
Listen up,
Most High Inquisitor!

I'll shut my mouth.
Not a single cry
will I let escape from my bitten-up lips.
Tie me to comets, like to horses' tails,
and race me out of here,

ripping me up on star bits.
Or here's what:
when my soul moves out,
frowning like a little idiot,
and exits to meet your judgment,
you
can put a gallows up over the Milky Way:
take me and string me up like a criminal.
Do what you want.
You could even quarter me.
I myself, as a righteous man, will wash your hands of it.
Only—
hear this!—
take away that cursed one,
the one you made my beloved!

I crumple miles of streets with the sweep of my paces.
Where am I to go, melting this hell!
In the mind of what divine Hoffmann
were you dreamt up, cursed woman?!

2

Both the sky
that's forgotten it's blue, with all the smoke,
and the clouds like flayed refugees,
I'll blast with the dawn of my final love,
bright like a consumptive's blush.

With joy I'll drown out the roar
of the horde
of those who have forgotten home and comfort.
People,
listen up!

Climb out of the trenches.
You can finish your fighting later.

Even if,
staggering off blood like Bacchus,
a drunken battle is raging—
even then, the words of love aren't defunct.
Dear Germans!
I know,
on your lips is
Goethe's Gretchen.

The Frenchman
dies happy on a bayonet,
and the shot-down aviator
crashes with a smile,
if only they remember
the kiss of your mouth,
Traviata.

But I'm in no mood for the rosy pulp
chewed up by centuries.
Lie down today at new feet!
You I sing,
my painted
redhead.

Perhaps of these days,
frightful as bayonet blades,
once the centuries have bleached my beard,
you and I will be all
that remains,
and I
will chase you from city to city.

You'll be given away in marriage across the sea,
trying to hide in night's burrow—
I'll kiss into you through the London fog
with the fiery lips of streetlamps.

In the heat of the desert you'll stretch out your caravans,
with lions standing guard—
beneath you
under the windblown sand,
I'll place my burning Sahara cheek.

You'll deposit a smile in your lips
as you watch—
the toreador is so handsome!
And suddenly I'll
fling my jealousy into the stands
through the dying eye of the bull.

If you should point your absentminded steps to a bridge
and think
how nice it would be to jump down—
It is I,
the Seine poured out underneath,
who will call to you,
baring my rotten teeth.

If, with another, you light up with horse-hoof fire
the Strelka or the Sokolniki,
then I, clambering way up above,
patient and naked, will torment you with moonlight.

I'm strong,
and soon they'll need me—

they'll command:
kill yourself in the war!
My last word will be
your name,
clotted on my shrapnel-shredded lips.

Will they give me a crown?
Or send me to Saint Helena?
I who have saddled the cloudbanks of life's storm
am an equal candidate
for tsar of the universe
and
the shackles.

If it's determined that I should be tsar,
then your dear little face
on the sunny gold of my coins
I'll order my people
to stamp!
But if I wind up
where the world fades into tundra,
where the river trades with the north wind,
then I'll scratch the name Lily onto my chains
and kiss them blind in the dark of the prison camp.

Listen up, you who've forgotten the sky's blue,
bristling all over
like animals!
This may very well be
the last love in the world,
lit up bright by a consumptive's blush.

3

I'll forget the year, the day, the date.
I'll lock myself up alone with a sheet of paper.
Come into creation, inhuman magic
of suffering-illuminated words!

Today, the moment I came in to see you,
I felt it—
something was wrong in the house.
You were hiding something in your silk dress,
and the smell of incense spread through the air.
Happy to see me?
In response, a cold
"Very."
The fence of reason is knocked down by confusion.
Burning and feverish, I pile up despair.

Listen here,
all the same
you can't hide the body.
Let the terrible word crash down on my head!
All the same
your every muscle,
as if in a megaphone,
trumpets:
She's dead, dead, dead!
No,
answer me.
Don't lie!
(How can I go back now, in my state?)
Like two graves
your eyes have sunken into your face.

The graves grow deeper.
There is no bottom.
It seems
I might fall from the scaffold of days.
I stretched my soul over the abyss like a tightrope,
and I totter there, juggling words.

I know
his love has worn you out.
I can read your boredom in so many signs.
Make yourself young again in my soul.
Acquaint your heart with the holiday of the body.

I know,
everyone pays for a woman.
That'll be fine
if for the moment,
instead of chic Paris dresses,
I can clothe you in tobacco smoke.

My love,
like an apostle in days of yore,
I'll carry down a thousand thousand roads.
For you in the ages a crown has been forged,
and in that crown are my words,
in a rainbow of convulsions.

Just as elephants, with their hundred-pound games,
sealed Pyrrhus's victory,
I thundered out your brain with the tread of a genius.
All in vain.
I can't tear you away.

Rejoice,
rejoice!

You've finished me off!
Now
my anguish is such
that I can only run to the canal
and shove my head into the water's bared teeth.

You gave me your lips.
How crude you were with them.
I touched them and went cold.
It was as if I were kissing, with my penitent lips,
a monastery carved from a frozen cliff.

The doors
slammed open.
He walked in,
splashed by the streets' merriment.
I
split in two, as it were, in my howl.
Yelled at him:
"Fine!
I'll go!
Fine!
She'll stay.
You can sew rags on her,
and her timid wings will fatten up in silk.
Watch out or she'll float away.
For a stone to weigh her down,
you can hang pearls around your wife's neck."

Oh, what a
night!
I myself pulled the despair tighter and tighter.
From my cries and my laughter
the room screwed up its ugly face in terror.

And like a vision, the image borne away from you rose,
your eyes shining down on the carpet,
as if some new Bialik had dreamt up
a blinding Queen of Hebrew Zion.

In torment
before the one I'd given up,
I, the kneeler, sank.
King Albert,
surrendering
all his cities,
was a birthday boy, compared to me.

Shine golden in the sun, you flowers and grasses!
Be springlike, lives of all the elements!
I only ask for poison—
to drink and drink in verse.

You who robbed my heart,
leaving it with nothing,
who tortured my soul into delirium,
accept this gift, my dear—
I may never come up with anything more.

Paint today's date like a holiday.
Come into creation,
magic equal to the Crucifixion.
You see,
I am nailed with words
to the paper.

1915

1 50,000,000
A Poem

150,000,000 is the name of the craftsman of this poem.
The bullet is its rhythm.
            Its rhyme, a fire spreading from building to building.
150,000,000 now speak through my lips.
This edition is printed
                    by rotary footsteps
on the cobblestone paper of squares.
Who would ask the moon,
                who could compel the sun to answer:
                        why do you cause all these
                                nights and days?
Who can name the ingenious author of the earth?
So
   of this
        my
            poem
                no one is the creator.
And it has only one idea—
                    to shine into the coming tomorrow.
This very year,
        on this day, at this hour,
                underground,
                    above ground,
                            through the sky,
                                and still higher,
there appeared the following
                    posters, placards, leaflets:

"EVERYONE!
            EVERYONE!
                        EVERYONE!
Everyone
who can't take any more!
Walk out
together
and march!"
                    (signed):
VENGEANCE—MASTER OF CEREMONIES.
HUNGER—MANAGING DIRECTOR.
BAYONET.
BROWNING.
BOMB.

            *(three
                        signatures
                                    of the secretaries)*

Let's go!
Letsgoletsgo!
Go, go,
go, go, go, go,
go, go!
It's all tumbling down!
            Vanka!
                        Stuff some Kerensky bucks in your sandal!
Think you can run off to the meeting barefoot?
Our sweet little Russia's had it!
                        They've ruined the poor girl!
We'll find a new Russia.
            A worldwide one!

Let's go-o-o-o-o-o!
There he sits, done up in gold,

                at tea

                    with petits fours.
I'll come to him

        as cholera.

             I'll come to him

                  as typhus.
I'll come to him,

        I'll tell him:

             "Wilson," I'll say,

                  "Woodrow,
you want a bucket of my blood?
You'll see . . ."

        We'll make it

            to Lloyd George himself,
and we'll tell him:

        "Listen here,

              Georgie . . ."
"Sure, you'll make it to him!

        He's across oceans.

        You think

          they're scared

             of some old Russian packhorse?"
"Not a bit of it!

        We'll go on our own two feet!"
Letsgoletsgo!
Roused by the call,

        from the forests,

           half awake,
a host of beasts and their young crept out.
A piglet crushed by an elephant squealed.
Puppies formed into puppy ranks.
Now, a human scream can be unbearable,

but the beasts' cry
                                tied your very soul in knots.
I will translate the animals' roar for you,
in case you don't know the language of beasts:
"Listen up,
                Wilson,
                                swimming in fatback!
If men are to blame,
                                then give them the punishment.
But we
                didn't sign any treaty in Versailles.
Why should we,
                the beasts,
                                have to go hungry?
Fellow beasts, fling your animal grief at Wilson!
Oh, to eat our fill just one more time!
Let's be off to Indias stuffed with tall grasses,
let's head for American pastures!"
O-o-o-h!
                We're so cramped in this cage of a blockade.
Forward march, automobiles!
                                To the meeting, motorbikes!
Step aside, small fries!
                Make way for the roads!
                                Road after road now falls into rank.
Listen to what the roads have to say.
                                Well, what is it they're saying?
"We've choked to death on winds and dust,
winding along rails through the starving steppe.
We're tired of trudging along behind convicts,
mile after flimsy, unpaved mile.
We want to pour out in asphalt,
settling down under the weight of express-lines.

Rise up!
          You've slept there long enough,
cradled by highway dust!
Let's go-o-o-o!"
E-e-e-e-e-e-e-e-e-e-e-e.
Let's go to the coalfields!
To get some bread!
                    Black bread,
                              baked just for us!
Only a fool
          would set off without fuel.
To the meeting, all you steam engines!
                              Steam engines,
                                        to the meeting!
Hur-r-r-r-r-r-y-y-y-y-y up!
                    Hurryhurry!
Hey,
     all you provinces,
                    break free from your anchors!
After Tula, Astrakhan,
                    huge bulk after bulk,
lands that have stood still
                    since Adam's day
set off,
     and advanced
together with others,
                    their cities giving off tiny rumbles.
Driving away the party-crashing darkness,
with lamps bumping forehead to forehead,
legions of firelight march to the meeting
with giant streetlamp strides.
And above,
          reconciling water with fire,

the drowned and festering seas rolled forward.
"Make way for the mischievous Caspian waves!
We won't change our course and head back to Russia!
Not in sorry little Baku,
                    but in exultant Nice,
with the Mediterranean we'll dance across beaches."
And finally,
            above the thunder
                        of running and vehicles,
heaving breath into the inordinate expanse of their lungs,
disheveled by clouds, they flew out of their caves
and set off like a storm—the winds of Russia.
Let's go-o-o-o!
Letsgoletsgo!
And all these
            one hundred fifty million people,
billions of fish,
            trillions of insects,
                        wild animals,
                                    house pets,
hundreds of provinces,
            with everything that was built
                        and stood
                                    or lived in them,
everything that could move,
        and everything that couldn't,
                everything that barely moved,
                            creeping,
                                crawling,   .
                                    swimming—
all of it burst forth like lava,
                    like lava!

And it buzzed above the place
                    where Russia once stood:
                         "Who gives a damn
                                   about the saccharine trade?
To pound to the clanging bells—that's what the heart desires!
Today
        we rush Russia
                    into paradise
through the rainbow-colored chinks in sunsets."
Go, go,
         go, go, go, go,
                         go, go!
Letsgoletsgo!
                 Through the white guard of snows!

Why is it that the carcasses of provinces have crawled away
from their age-old, governor-approved zones?
What is it that the heavens gape their ears to hear?
Who is that, illuminated by the horizon?
Today
        the eyes
              of the world
                         turn to us
and all ears strain
                 to pick up our every sound,
in order to see this sight,
in order to listen to these words:
this is the will
              of the revolution,
                              cast beyond the final barrier,
this is the meeting
              that has amassed
                          into one giant lump of machine bodies

the carcasses of men and beasts;
this
    is hands,
              paws,
                    claws,
                          levers,
all thrust
        into the rarified air
in sworn allegiance.
Forget all those poets
                who only try to howl more celestially,
and listen instead
            to these songs:
We've come through capitals,
    we've broken through tundras,
        we've marched across mud and enormous puddles.
We've come in our millions,
            millions of laborers,
                    millions of workers and servants.
We've come from apartments,
            we've escaped from warehouses,
                  from arcades lit up by flames.
We've come in our millions,
            millions of things—
                    disfigured,
                        broken,
                            in ruins.
We've come down from the mountains,
        we've crawled out of the forest,
                out of fields gnawed on by years.

We've come
        in our millions,
                millions of livestock—
                                wild,
                                        dim-witted,
                                                and starving.
We've come
            in our millions,
                    godless ones,
                            pagans,
                                and atheists—
banging
        our foreheads,
                    rusty iron,
                        and the ground;
all of us
now pray devoutly
to the Lord our God.
Come out,
            but not from some tender
                                bed of stars,
God of iron,
            fiery God,
God not of Neptunes,
                Vegas, and Mars,
but God made of meat—
                God-man!
Not driven up high
onto the stars' seashores,
but earthly,
            among us,
come out—
        appear!

Not the one
          "who art in heaven."
We ourselves,
in full view of everyone,
today
     will
          work
               miracles.
To fight
in your name,
in the thunder,
               in the smoke,
we stand up on our hind legs.
We're trying for a feat
                    three times harder than God's;
he created
          by just tossing stuff into a void.
We,
     as we build up something new, can't just sit
and fantasize—
               we've also got to dynamite the old.
Thirst, give us water!
Hunger, fill us up!
It's time
          to bear
our body into battle.
Bullets, fill the air!
Rake over the timid!
In the thicket of stragglers,
ring out, Parabellum!
That's it!
From the bottom of your souls!

With heat,
                with burning,
                                with iron,
                                        with light,
cook,
        burn,
                cut,
                        raze!
Our legs
            are lightning-fast trains whizzing by.
Our arms
            are fans blowing dust from the fields.
Our fins are steamships.
Our wings, an airplane.
March!
        Fly!
                Swim!
                        Roll!—
checking the register of the whole universe.
If a thing is necessary—
                        that's good,
                                it'll come in handy.
If it's unnecessary—
                    to hell with it!
                                Just cross it out.
We'll
        finish you off,
                    world-romantic!
Instead of faith,
                in our soul
                        we've got steam
                                and electricity.
No beggars here!
                We'll pocket the wealth of all worlds!

If it's old, kill it.
                Use their skulls as ashtrays!
Washing away the old
in a wild rout,
we'll thunder a new myth
over the world.
We'll kick down
the fence of time.
We'll gamma a thousand rainbows
across the sky.
The roses and dreams defiled by poets
                    will be revealed in a new light.
Everything
       will be a joy
            to our eyes—
                the eyes of overgrown children!
We may just decide
           to come up with
                new roses—
the roses of capitals surrounded by petals of town squares.
Everyone
       branded
           with the stamp of torment,
come to the feet of today's executioner.
And you
       will discover
           that people
              can be tender,
like the love
       climbing up a ray of light to a star.
Our soul
       will be the confluence
              of Volgas of love.

Anyone
          who floats to us
will be washed by our shining eyes.
Down every
               fine artery
                              we'll let sail
the fantastic ships of poetic inventions.
As we have written,
so shall the world be:
on Wednesday,
                 in the past,
                                today,
                                     and forever,
and tomorrow,
                 and further,
                                world without end!
Fight
      for a hundred-year
                           summer,
                                  and sing:
"Let this be
            the final
                      and decisive battle!"
Through a hail of throats we'll thunder our hymn!
A million plus!
               Multiplied by a hundred!
In the streets!
               On the rooftops!
                                For the sun!
Let loose into worlds
                      the songlegged gymnasts of words!
And Russia
          is no longer

                a beggar in rags,
                            or some heap of debris,
                                        or the ashes of buildings—
all
    of Russia
                is a single Ivan,
and his
            arm
                is the Neva,
his heels, the Caspian steppe.
Let's go!
Letsgoletsgo!
Not walking, but flying!
Not flying, but striking like lightning,
rinsing our souls with zephyrs.
Walk straight past
                        all the bars and banyas.
Beat, drum!
            Drum, drum!
There once were slaves!
                            No slaves anymore!
Baarbeat!
        Baarbanya!
                    Ba-am-bam!
Hey, chests-of-steel!
                    Strongmen, hey!
Beat, drum!
            Drum, beat!
Either—or.
All or nothing.
We will win!
            We're winning!
                        We've won!

On the drum!
                On the drum!
                                On the drum!
The revolution
                will strip the tsar of his tsar's title.
The revolution
                will fling the crowds' hunger at every bakery.
But what sort of name
                will we give to you,
all of Russia, whirlwinded up into a pillar?!
The Council of Commissars
                                is just a tiny part of Ivan's brain—
its decrees can't keep up with his gallop.
His heart is so big and cumbersome
that even Lenin could hardly shake it up.
You can force a Red Army soldier to retreat
or squeeze a communist into a prison yoke,
but how do you fence in
                someone like this
once
        someone like this
                        takes a step?!
Thunder tore up the seashores' ears,
and splashes shot up all over the land,
when Ivan,
                his heavy steps raining down,
set off
        like a storm to stun the universe.
We'll strap our feet into the stirrups of fantasy,
throw a saddle over the gunpowder of days,
and blast off
                after this blinding vision,
to radiate through the world's limitless spaces.

Now
  let's give the wheel of inspiration a spin.
Measure out our rhythm anew.
The main character of this chapter is Wilson.
The place of action is America.
The world,
    gathering up a continental
           quintet,
bestowed upon it a power most magical.
A city there stands
      on a single screw,
entirely electro-dynamo-mechanical.
In Chicago
    there are fourteen thousand streets—
         the sunbeams of town squares.
From each of them
     seven hundred alleys branch off,
        as long as a train travels in a year.
How chic it is in Chicago!
In Chicago,
  it's so bright
     that the sun
       seems no better than a halfpenny candle.
In Chicago,
    even for raising eyebrows
          they've got
            electrical current.
In Chicago,
   miles
     up into the sky,
       the steel circus acrobats of roads
          skip and jump.
 How chic it is in Chicago!

In Chicago,
                every inhabitant
                            has no less than a general's rank.
And their work
            is to booze it up
                        in bars, without cares
                                    or burdens.
Oh, what foods
                they've whipped up
                            in the bars of Chicago!
How chic it is in Chicago!
How chic it is!
                And how marvelous!
In Chicago
            there's such a raging din,
that a cargo transport
                    with a thousand-power motor
seems
        like a crumb floating by on the wind;
it seems
            to rustle past as quiet as a mouse.
The train won't carry
Russians
            into the city;
not for us are the palaces' many floors.
I alone have been there;
I alone ate and drank in the bars,
tossing back gin with the Yanks.
They may let you in, too,
                        but until they do,
you can still stuff yourselves full of wonders:
in my speed-skate lines,
in the boots of my lines,
walk across America yourselves!

An aerostation
                    parked on top of a skyscraper.
Step right in,
                    squeezing side by side in the dirigible!
From up here the bridges look like sparrows' ribs.
And Chicago below
                    is like a toad on the ground.
And later,
          from up in the sky,
                              barely visible,
breaking loose,
              we drop down like a stone into the abyss.
Through a tunnel
in the metro
              we root up underground miles
and exit to a square.
                    Overflowing with people.
About three miles wide.
Here begins just what we need—
a "royal road,"
              or as they say,
                              "King Street."
What kind of street is it?
What can you find there?
Why, there you can find
                    The Cheeple Strong Hotel.
But is it a hotel
              or some kind of dream?
In this hotel,
          wrapped in cleanliness
                              and warmth,
Woodrow
          Wilson
              himself lives.

What sort of building it is, I can't tell you.

When I do tell you,

I humbly ask you not to believe me.
There is no place to which you could retreat
in order to get a view of the whole thing.
What

you can see

is just one little corner,
but even it

is a marvel!
Take a look, for example,

at that bit of trellis,
forged from condensed sunlight.
And if you try to walk around it,

you'd swear it was a mountain!
Covering hundreds of miles,

maybe thousands.
Its weathervanes extend into seventh heaven,
polished

by God himself.
There's also a stairway,

but you could never ascend it!
Winding between columns,

balconies,

porticos,
there's no telling
how many steps it contains—
a hell of a lot

of steps!
If you're going on foot,

you'd better start young;
you still might not make it

in your old age!

As for the elevators,
                  they stop at taverns along the way,
so you don't have to go hungry.
And once we've arrived—
              if they're happy to see us—
they'll let us through the front door in fives.
First the guests walk through three hundred rooms.
Finally they get past them.
           Whew!
Here
again the rooms start up.
You're met by a lackey.
A baton in his fist.
You pass five more such lackeys.
Another baton.
         Another lackey.
You get through that hall,
           and there's another lackey.
Past all the lackeys
       the couriers
          run even thicker.
Courier racing after courier in full career.
Countless couriers.
        Their number would make
Khlestakov, that puppy, gasp for breath.
And only
     when you're worn out
           by the terrible bustle,
when
    it no longer seems
        you'll ever get out,
and it seems
     there's no reason to think

it will ever end—
                    you see the reception room.
From here on in, it's easy:
a seven-foot-tall
secretary stands mute in the doorway.
We crack open the door.
Up the steps—(two of them)—
we go,
        take a peek,
                    and gasp—
That's not the afternoon sun in your eyes,
but Wilson's gigantic top hat
rising up like Sukharev Tower.
He spits dynamite
and belches,
red all over,
                    bursting with bravado.
You take a look at his girth—
a Yorkshire pig, if ever there was one!
While his height—
                    well, you can't say how tall he his,
so far removed from his feet is his head!
Whether he's loaded with something,
                            or whistling through his teeth,
every sound he makes
                    is like the bang of a cannon.
People are nothing,
                    they walk around beneath him,
standing there
            like little huts.
His cheeks are of such
                    supernatural fleshiness

that they call out to you—
                              come
                              and lie down!
His clothing is thin,
                    as if it weren't there at all,
spun from the finest poetic bliss.
Wilson's long johns
                    are not long johns, but a sonnet—
a six-foot swath of America's version of *Onegin*.
And how hard he works!
                              He never once takes a break.
You'd think he'd work himself to death.
He twists one giant finger
                              around another,
twisting now faster,
                    now slower.
One little twist,
              and there's a layoff
                              at some factory.
They don't want to pay me
                    my per-line fee.
Another twist,
              and the Strausses strike up their waltzes
as a rain of gold pours into the palace.
They spare no expense
                    to keep Wilson fed.
He's stuffed full of food
                    and drink.
And in case he should die,
                              so the body doesn't go to waste,
fat-renderers are standing by,
                              oil refineries at the ready.
All Americans
              are offered up to him,

even as they
proudly declare:
                   I am an
                           American subject.
I am a
        free
            American citizen.
His swarms of servants
                       stand
                              bowing below him.
The whole hall is full
                      of Lincolns,
                               Whitmans,
                                       Edisons.
He's got a bevy
              of beauties
                         of the most selective nobility.
They hang on his minutest movement.
Have you heard
              of Adelina
Patti?
      She's here, too!
Whitman stands ready, in a tight-fitting tuxedo,
to rock back and forth in an unprecedented rhythm.
In possession of the very highest American rank—
"Distinguished Smoother of Ladies' Wrinkles"—
already made-up and wearing a hat,
Chaliapin is ready to belt out a tune at any time.
Littering the parquet floors with sand,
professors crumbling away from old age stand.
Most renowned of them all, Mechnikov himself
stands there trimming the candles' charred wicks.
Perhaps
        the scholars

were brought here
by the theory of the flood?
The artists,
by some sort of
glorious
école-des-beaux-arts?
Nothing of the kind!
The only reason
they
came
is to go to the bazaar.
Every morning,
all these
favorites of the muses and fame
load up with baskets
and head for the market,
then carry home
various
butters
and meats.
Longfellow, the king of the poets,
I guess,
drags off a hundred jars of cream.
And Wilson gobbles,
getting fatter and fatter,
his stomachs expanding,
adding floor after floor.

A Little Note:
Artists paint
Wilsons,
Lloyd Georges,
Clemenceaus—

all with bewhiskered
                    or whiskerless mugs—
and it's no use:
                    they
are all
        one and the same.

Now
    we've had enough laughing chapters.
In your heads
        you can picture
                America clearly.
We move on now
        to the main event.
To the unbelievable,
            to the gigantic gist.
That
        day
            must have been
                        fireproof.
Lands fell silent in an outpouring of heat.
The winds' jagged-toothed harrows
struggled in vain to break up the air.
In Chicago
            the heat was exorbitant:
about 100 degrees,
                or 80 for sure.
Everyone was at the beach.
Those who could went for a walk,
                        while a majority were just lying there.
The sweat
            smelled sweet
                        on their well-groomed bodies.

They walked around panting.
                              They lay there panting.
Ladies led little pugs around on leashes,
and
    the pugs
              were fattened up
                              like calves.
One grande dame,
                  nodding off in her idyll,
had a heat-stricken moth
                          fly right into her nostril.
Some were indulging in lively discussions,
                                  saying "ah,"
                                          saying "ooh."
Fuzz flew from the trees,
from the mimosa trees.
It showed pink
        on the fine white muslins and silks
                          and white on the pink ones.
And so
for a rather long time
everyone was engaged
in pleasant pastimes.
But within
an hour or so,
certain things
had begun
to change.
There was something scarcely audible—
you could, perhaps, sense it with the tippy-tip of your soul—
something like a breath of wind.
Splashes spread out
                  over the calm sea.

What is it?

        What's going on?

The next morning,

            in a flash of lightning,

the ATA

        (the American Telegraph Agency)

                shot out over the city through the radio:

"A terrible storm over the Pacific Ocean.

        The monsoons and trade winds have lost their minds.

On the Chicago coast, some fish have been caught.

             Very strange fish.

                  Furry.

                      With big noses."

Sleepy people crawled out of their houses

            and hadn't yet discussed the event,

while the radio

        kept on posting

            urgent announcements:

"The fish were a lie.

        A local fisherman was drunk.

The monsoons and trade winds are right where they should be.

        But there is a storm.

            It's even more terrible.

                Causes unknown."

Large ships blocked all the ports,

        joined

           by

            tiny little steamship companies.

The dollar fell.

        Suitcases sold like hotcakes.

           The stock market was in a panic.

Strangers

    stopped strangers

on the street:
                    "Got any inside information?"
Special edition!
            On the radio!
                        Extra! Extra! Special edition!
"The radiogram was garbled.
                    The thunder isn't from any storms.
It's something else:
                the roar of enemy squadrons."
Radios were put up all over.
                        And, invalidating the previous,
soon came
            the new,
                    the final,
                        the breathtaking,
                                    the sensational:
"It's not cannon smoke,
                    but the blue of the ocean.
There are no battleships,
                    no fleets,
                        no squadrons.
                            Zilch. Nothing.
                                There's only Ivan."

What Ivan?
Which Ivan?
Where Ivan?
Why Ivan?
How Ivan?
There's never been a more confused situation,
without a single trustworthy,
                        sensible
                            explanation.
The crown council immediately convened.
All night the lights in the palace knew no peace.

Wilson's minister,
                    Arthur Krupp,
talked till he nearly
                    dead-down-dropped.
Capitalism's faithful treasure,
Creusot himself was completely exhausted.
Wilson
        displayed
                    extraordinary
                              persistence,
and toward morning
                    decided—
                              "I'll take him on single-handed."
Disaster approaches.
                It's two thousand miles out.
                        Now a thousand.
                                Now a hundred.
                                        And . . .
Outlines of the figure drawing near
                    were felt,
                          noticed,
                              seen by wide-eyed lighthouses.

Lines
    of this chapter,
              thunder out,
                      using rhythm to burrow through time!
Resurrect them in song—
the myth of Homer's heroes,
                      the story of Troy,
inflated beyond recognition!
Starving,
        my heat set at a single degree,

I rejoice at life
    as at a favor
bestowed,
following your legendary progress, Ivan.
Where to now?
     Where will you plant your feet?
Across what seas will you march?
We'll frame the lightning of breaking dispatches
in this cold verse chapter.
Ivan's running start burst into the Dardanelles.
Turks beheld
    with mouths
agape:
  a man,
     his head as high as Kazbek,
was walking right over the Dardanelles forts.
Old men slipped away.
      The young headed for the pier.
They came out,
    singing songs of rebellion and youth.
And the moment
     the swell swept onto the shore,
the moment the wave reached the pier—
they leapt,
   as if at a long-awaited signal,
man upon man,
    class upon class.
Some people were crowned
      and others, driven off.
They skipped across the sea
      and disappeared from view.
Others were swallowed up in the bathtub of the sea,
and still others
    became food for blood-boozing sharks;

but some
            made it in,
                        tumbled into Ivan
and settled inside him
                        like sailors in a stateroom.
(Meanwhile, in Chicago,
                        nothing yet foretold
a difficult time ahead for the Chicagoans.
Bending in arcs,
                        thrusting out their sides,
they had a grand old time
                        tearing along in mad dances.)
The Romans stood stock still
                        as a storm raged on the Tiber.
The Tiber itself,
                        rising up in a fury,
shaved the Pope's head clean
and went off through the morning lume to join Ivan.
(Meanwhile, in Chicago,
                        mustaches were taking a dip in liqueurs
while some female protuberance of meat got fondled—
"Ee-la-la!
            Oh-la-la!"
 kissy-faced,
            buck naked,
                        rambunctious.)
It was the blackest of nights,
                        without any star streetlamps.
Tripping across masses of water
                        to join Wilson,
the Rhine crowned by poets
                        sneaked away,
shining just a tad, like a light-blue trouser stripe.

(Chicago
        slept,
            all danced out
                    and drunk,
pampering its pudgy body with pillows.
The blue mist fell asleep.
                    You could hear it breathing,
the sea snoring and snoring away.
Day rose.
        Would it bring retribution?)
Ivan advanced,
            shining like the dawn.
Ivan strode forward,
                kicking up surf.
Living things ran.
                Ran along the coasts.
The world swaggered redly like a volcano.
Only there is no such volcano
on the map drawn up by old geographers.
The entire universe,
                not some pathetic little Etna—
a crater spewing out nations like lava.
Bellowing as they rushed
                    across erased countries,
the living and dead fled
                from the downpour of lava.
Some ran to Ivan
            with outstretched
arms,
        others to Wilson in a headlong dash.
From the everyday slime of petty facts,
one came to light and stood out:
suddenly
        all middles had been destroyed—

there was no middle ground left on earth.
No colors,
        no shades,
                nothing remained—
besides
one color staining everything white,
and another
                bloodying everything with the color of blood.
Everything crimson got more and more crimson.
The white, ever whiter and whiter.
Ivan
     walked on blood
                across kingdoms,
celebrating jubilees of fire over the world.
It turned out they built all those fortresses in vain.
Shut up, you babbling cannons!
                    That'll do!
Over impregnable Gibraltar he passed.
And the world
                like an ocean sprawled out before Ivan.
(Meanwhile, in Chicago,
                at the beach,
                    a litter of sluts
was alarmed by the sea's frenzy.
Time sent forth rumor after rumor,
letting loose the reins of tall tales.)
What sort of admiral
                awash on the open sea
could so clearly understand the world's waterways?!
He walked,
                stuffed chock full of the dynamite of people.
He walked,
                ready to explode with the whole world's malice.

In all four directions spread

the lap of the Pacific.

Ivan,

with no map

and no compass needle,

walked

with his goal unwavering before him,

as if

the sea spread wide before him,

were nothing but a tiny dinner plate.

(Meanwhile, in Chicago,

a wave rolled right up

to Wilson,

a wave sent forth by Ivan's walking.

Wilson summoned his archers,

boxers,

and fencers,

to build up his strength for the battle.)

Ivan beamed like discoverers,

he beamed like Columbuses

when the smell

of land

carried

to his nose,

as if

from a thousand-scented flower bed.

(Meanwhile, in Chicago,

the boxers

nearly burst from their labor.

They laid Wilson out flat on the ground,

and with a

"Get to it, boys!"

they spread,

massaged,

and rubbed him down with special ointments for strength.)
A lighthouse's monogaze pierced the eyes—
and then,
                    invading brains,
                                    eyes,
                                        and mouths,
climbing out of every ocean trench,
America kept right on advancing.
Dockyard took a running jump upon dockyard.
Viaduct flew over viaduct.
There was such hideous smoke
                        that with a newfound belief in the devil,
you walked around convinced
                            you were in hell.
(Where was Wilson's flab?
                        They huffed and puffed it right off!
Made him look forty years younger.
His muscles swelled like stomachs.
The trainers patted him down.
                            Yes, sir.
                                He's ready.)
Ivan arrived,
    frothing the waves into foam,
                    sending it right over the giant houses' roofs,
Ivan stepped out onto the shore
                        in America,
                            dry as a bone,
                                right down to his feet.

(They fastened onto Wilson the very last rivet
of his mechanical armor,
raised the helmet over his brow,
and he shot off at a run to meet Ivan.)

Chicagoans
        don't like
               to squeeze together
                      in crowded streets.
And anyway,
        the squares
              in Chicago
                 are the very best.
But an inordinately large square—
                    even
                       for the Chicagoans—
was prepared specially for this event.
The people
        surrounding the field of battle—
never mind if it was inordinate!—
                   split into two groups.
On one side,
        in ermines
              and beaver furs,
on the other,
        shining blue in greasy work shirts.
Horses too
        were thrown into
              the mix:
with the fur-coats,
            an Arabian racing stallion;
and with the grease-shirts,
              the heavy hulks of carthorses.
The workhorses shot out a few neighs,
             talking some horsey trash to the stallion.
Automobiles too
        were gathered together,
                slipping and sliding on oil—

imports
        and exports
                divvied up by class.
The fur-coats
             were joined by an elegant limousine,
the grease-shirts
                by
                  a massive, hundred-power truck.
No exception was made
                  for poetry or paints;
the battle, a most stern judge,
                    would decide their fate, too.
To the fur-coats
             went the lines of the whole world's decadents.
To the grease-shirts,
                the Futurists' iron lines.
No one,
        not a soul, would avoid retribution—
even
      the stars
            couldn't escape.
Go to the fur-coats,
             you constellation-generals;
to the grease-shirts,
             all you millions of the Milky Way!
Letting out to the surface its icebound avalanches,
the very globe of the earth
split into two hemispheres,
and, holding still,
             dangled from the sun
                like a scale.
All the cannons
          above the square

boomed out:
"It's time for the Championship
of Worldwide Class Struggle!"
Wilson's gate
                    was about
                                  a mile wide,
                                              but even so,
he had to turn sideways
                        and barely got through it.
With his enormous boots
                          he crumpled the concrete
and thundered out
                    with his clanking metal.
He stared at Ivan as he entered the arena,
to look over his enemy,
                        but it's no use
                                    staring.
                                    Wilson had to admit:
                                              Ivan was well built,
the color of his body showing through his shirt.
One contestant
                    had revolvers
                                  with four triggers,
a saber
        bent into seventy blades,
while the other
                had only
                          his two bare hands,
one of which
                was even tucked under his belt.
Wilson looked Ivan up and down.
                                  A giggle crossed his whiskers.
He shrugged up his epaulets' stitching.

"The very idea that I—

oh Lord!—

this is the guy?

That I

couldn't handle

this guy?!"

And it seemed

a funeral mound was piling up

to the intertwined howling of the winds.

He'll lie down in his coffin,

and from this day forth,

no one

will ever

hear anything more

about our Ivan.

Wilson's saber screamed.

From Ivan's shoulder

downward,

it must have sliced three solid miles.

Wilson stood and waited—

there should have been blood,

but from

the wound,

suddenly a man

popped out.

And they kept right on coming!

People,

buildings,

battleships,

horses

all clambered through the narrow incision.

They came out singing,

all in music.

What a disaster!
    They've sent from their northern Troy
a man-horse stuffed with rebellion!
The Chicagoans ran around,
                spreading the news
of the Soviet formation through their own dumbstruck ranks.

Comrade newspapermen,
                don't bother trying to find out
whether and where
                this battle took place.
In this chapter,
                concentrated into five minutes,
are all the years of battles real and imagined.
Not to Lenin is my poignant verse dedicated.
In battle
I glorify millions,
        I see millions,
and so it's the millions I sing.
Listen up, you historians and orators,
to one who's witnessed the upheavals of battles unreal!
"Rise up, you who have been branded with the curse!"—
the joyful news shot out.
In answer,
        the voice of millions
rang out:
    "All set!"
                "Yes, sir!"
"God save Wilson!
Powerful, supreme":
they too
raised their rusty voice in answer.

Half the earth belted out a red song.
The other half, a white.
And then,
                after the song of red,
and then,
                after the white one, too—
battering rams slammed at the future's barred doors,
and a stubble of rays began to scratch
                                and sweep.
Hands grew thicker,
                easily untangling
unknown dimensions of soul and earth.
Lashed by the birch switches of rebellion,
shop owners,
                without bothering to finish their trade,
spread at a run, like a scalded anthill,
from every bank
                and store
                        and office.
Onto the choking embankments and dikes,
toward the cities
                from the oceans,
                                waters advanced.
Telegraph poles, now here,
                        now there,
strung up cathedrals with their wires.
Tearing free from their familiar foundations,
skyscraper after skyscraper set off,
and, the way a tiger in a zoo
                        eats meat
                                by the pound,
scarfed down smaller buildings with the maws of their gates.
Yanking themselves right out of the pavement—
"Well then, boss man, where's your monstrous forehead?"—

into the mirrored windows of jewelry stores,
cobblestones flung themselves.
Without any fear of running aground,
not afraid to tear their plump bodies on church towers,
simply—
            just like you and I would—
whales walked across dry land.
Everything red
                and everything white
was fighting,
                fighting and singing.
Out in the courtyard, Wilson
                            was dancing a cakewalk,
twisting his front and his backside,
but before his foot could finish the equivoque,
Wilson looked to the door
                    and saw:
unflinching,
                marching forward at an ominous pace,
man after man,
            thing after thing
barged through the door:
"Mister Wilson,
                if you please, we call you to account!"
And then,
            after all this time pretending to be good,
ladies' necklaces
                attacked Wilson
                                like cobras.
Trying to pick
                the softest and cleanest,
massive trucks
            chased billionaires' wives
                                through their living rooms.

There's no escape!
Furniture, the forty-legged beast,
set a trap.
It trampled people with its massive wardrobes,
skewered them on table legs.
Across Rockefellers
lolling about facedown,
their throats
pinched tight by their own shirt-collars,
trampling them
like cockroaches,
the rebellious furniture ran out
and disappeared into Chicago.
On the streets,
from seven feet away
you couldn't make out a building through the thick battle-smoke.
The way it sometimes happens with a cinematograph,
all of a sudden,
up close,
you would see
through the chaos:
rearing up on its hind legs,
the Council of the People's Economy
deals a *coup de grâce* to crawling speculation.
But Wilson wouldn't give up:
he took a seat in the yard,
pressed on some kind of golden springs,
and a line of troops formed up,
Wilson's division of inhuman armed forces.
More terrible than tanks
or whole platoons of soldiers,
stomachless it rose,
hundred-mouthed it set out,

million-toothed
                    it marched—Hunger.
Hunger gnaws, and you crack like a nut.
It shoveled off a village, crunching the bones in its teeth.
And people,
            people and beasts alike,
                        it popped by the handful into its mouth.
In front of Hunger,
                    Ruin advances,
clearing a path, its ears pricked up in alert.
If industry so much as breathes,
                            Ruin will hear it.
Ruin can hear every factory breathe.
It bangs on the factory,
                    and the factory falls down.
It squeezes industry,
                    and industry is reduced to rubble.
It smashes railroads to smithereens as if with a club.
Everything is destroyed,
                    perishes,
                        collapses.
Get ready!
        Attack!
            Really try, now!
                    Sweat!
Hunger's throat,
            Ruin's gullet
                    we'll squeeze shut
                            in a noose of railroads!
And at the moment when all the world's airflow was cut off,
pinched shut by Hunger,
then,
        swinging its battering ram of trains,
Transport moved to the fore.

The gray beards of its steamships flapped in the wind.
They fought,
                    and soon Hunger had to surrender,
and right on top of it,
                              gobbling up its remains,
our trains passed, loaded with grain.
Woodrow
            squirmed,
                        and having angrily
belted out the order,
                        "Crush them this very second,"
he sent out another swarm of warriors—
the deadliest infections known to man.
They marched, chained to their dirty armor—
spirochete on top of spirochete,
                                    vibrio on vibrio.
With the poison of bacteria,
                            through the paws of lice,
they polluted our blood,
                            going straight for the throat.
Unprecedented diseases
                    appeared:
suddenly
        a person
                would start to feel sleepy,
then he'd break out in pustules,
then swell up,
                and finally burst like a mushroom.
Against them advanced,
                        led by a rainbow-eyed
                                                drugstore,
infirmaries,
            clinics,
                    and hospitals,

blasting bottles of carbolic out their windows.
The lice retreated
                          and bunched together in a swarm.
Then the lice were shot
                          point-blank
                                      by a microscope.
Disinfectant hammered and hammered with its flail.
The enemies fell,
                          pulling up their little legs.
And up above,
                          flapping its prescription-flag,
the People's Health Commissariat took a victory lap.
A moan tore itself out of Wilson—
his diseases and Hunger had been defeated,
and so he sent out his final army—
the toxic army of ideas.
Democratisms,
                 humanisms—
ism after ism
                 advanced.
Before you could figure out
                          what was good for you,
your head
          was Talmuddied
                          by philosophy.
They engulfed you in a slime of romances,
bewitched you with singing,
                          and lured you with pretty paintings.
Loading
          their empty heads
                          with books
for ballast,
          professor after professor advanced.

They were met
                    by a young crowd,
and into the funnel of Browning muzzles
disappeared Roman law
along with various others.
Pulling the wool over the people's eyes,
scaring them with hell,
                              enticing them with heaven,
some bald as your knee,
                          some shaggy like beasts,
with their Gospels of faith
                            and their superstitious charms,
kicking up dust with their robes,
an army of black-and-white priests advanced.
Beneath a hail of decrees
                          from the red avalanche,
they scattered—
                priests,
                        mullahs,
                                rabbis.
Well then, wonderworkers,
                          why don't you try to arise
from your deathbeds!
                      On the field of bloody contest
the support of faith came crashing down—
                                          Peter
and the cracked-open head of his cathedral.
At that point,
              Wilson's poets flew into the sky
to shoot down from above like airplanes.
With the bait
              of an academic ration
we lured them,
                waiting until they dropped down.
Wilson's poets hurled themselves, dropping like stones,

and got straight to it,
                    plucking the feathers of rhyme!
Into their *Collected Works,*
                        like underground burrows,
the classics retreated,
                    but we showed them no mercy!
In vain
        did
            Gorky,
                    like a hen on her eggs,
shield them,
                spreading thin his worn-out authority.
Sweeping over miles with the farms of their feet,
clearing paths with the faucets of their hands,
the Futurists
                routed the past,
releasing culture's confetti to the winds.
Wall against wall,
                    wallowing in dust,
the worthless Louvre
                    fought with the Admiralty,
until
    on the bayonet
                    of the Admiralty's spire,
the Louvre's painting-guts were strung up.
The final skirmish.
                    Wilson himself.
And the Wilsonites watched in horror—
he was instantly reduced to ashes
when he tried to crush the sun with his ass.
Who now remembers the names of those commanders in chief
who piled up victory after victory?
Crashing and rumbling in an international Tsushima,
the old order's fleet sank straight into the deep.
Trampling the corpse of the past with factories,

the future bawled out through a trillion smokestacks:
"Whether you call us Abel
                              or Cain,
we couldn't care less!
The future is here!
                              The future is victorious!
Hey, you ages,
                go cap in hand!"
The horizon spitefully made way for the sun.
And having just
                    sold out half the world,
Cain, that genius, grabbed hold of a ray,
the way a musician lays his hands on the keyboard.

History,
        your fast current shows clearly
                                in this chapter.
Starving and aching,
the cities make way,
                        and above the dust of their avenues,
like a sun it rises: another existence.
A year with interminable zeroes.
                              A holiday not indicated
                                    on any church calendar.
Everything's decked out in flags,
                              both people
                                    and buildings.
Maybe it's the hundredth anniversary
                              of the October Revolution,
or maybe everyone
                is just
                        in one hell of a good mood.
Driving dirigibles up the heavens' gradient,

like trains
                on the decks of innumerable squadrons,
through the twists and bends of pedestrian columns,
cadre after cadre of humans form ranks.
With their big heads,
                and glowing bright red,
just down from Mars, the Martians join in.
An airplane leaps up
                and then disappears,
and once again it shows dark against the sun like a bird.
And they keep on arriving
                        from the most remote planets,
their propellers fanning out from behind the sun.
Deserts have long been washed from the face of the world,
while trees sprout spectacular trunk after trunk.
On a square of greenery
                in the former Sahara,
this day
        marks an annual celebration.
Day after day, the days descended,
and again the dark of night grew thick.
Before they were even finished lining up,
                                the congregation
burst forth:
        "Let's begin!"
"Voices of people,
                beasts' voices,
                        the rivers' mighty roar—
we weave you all together ever higher in our song of praise.
Everyone sing and everyone listen
                        to the world's solemn requiem.
To you, from long ago,
                who starved through years
trumpeting the news of today's paradise,

to you,
            who provided us
food,
        drink,
                and song
                        for a millionennium.
To you women,
                    born under ermine
mantles,
            then dressing your body in rags
and falling in a dead faint
                            as you waited for bread
in unfathomable lines.
To you,
        legions of frail-boned children,
crowds of youth bent over in hunger,
those who lived to see something,
                            and those
who didn't live long enough to see anything.
To you,
        beasts
                with your ribs showing,
who have forgotten about the oats eaten up by people,
who labored, carrying someone or something,
until, whipped to death, you collapsed completely.
To you,
        executed on the barricades of the spirit
so that the present day might be sung,
who heard the future coming with your insatiable ears,
you painters,
                singers,
                        and poets.
To you, who,
            through the smoke and the fumes,

with your lives barely clinging on, by an iota,
gnashing through rusty iron and gears,
still kept on working,
                          still kept on doing.
To you we raise unceasing words of glory,
every year blooming, never fading,
you who were tortured for our sake; glory to you,
you millions of living,
                          brick,
                                    and other assorted Ivans."
The worldwide parade dispersed smoothly—
bygone grief doesn't trouble the soul for long.
Through the years,
                          sorrow
                                    is orchestrated into peace
and flung up to shoot through the sky as a song.
The echoes of voices are ringing still
about some people's deaths,
                                    about eternal remembrance,
while the people
                          in their many
                                    shining streets
are rolling through their minute of bright joy.
Well, keep right on rolling to your song's tune—
blossom, earth, as you reap and sow.
It's for you,
                the bloody Iliad of revolutions!
The Odyssey of hungry years is for you!

1919–1920

The Way It Usually Goes

Everyone who gets born is granted some love,
but between work,
income,
and the like,
from day to day
the heart's soil dries and hardens.
The heart is dressed in a body;
the body, in a shirt—
but that wasn't enough!
One guy—
the idiot!—
made up a bunch of cuffs for his shirts
and decided to pour starch all over his breast.
They all change their tune as old age approaches.
The woman packs on cosmetics.
The man, following Müller, waves his arms like a windmill.
But it's too late.
The skin teems with wrinkles.
Love blooms for a while,
a little while—
and then shrivels.

As a Boy

I too was given my fair share of love.
But starting in childhood,
the rank and file
are drilled for various labors.
Whereas I

would run off to the banks of the Rioni
and mosey about,
not doing a damn thing.
Mama would get mad:
"What a rotten little boy!"
Papa threatened to whip me with his belt.
But I,
raking in a counterfeit three-ruble note,
would play Three Leaves with the soldiers by the fence.
Unburdened by shirts,
without any shoey burden,
I'd roast all day in the heat of Kutaisi.
I'd turn to the sun now my back,
now my belly,
until my stomach started growling.
The sun stared and marveled:
"You can barely see him down there!
But he too
has a heart.
He's doing his best!
How
does he find room
in that
tiny little space
for me,
the river,
and the towering cliffs?!"

As a Youth

Youth is filled with a bunch of pursuits.
We teach grammar worse than any fool.
I even got myself kicked out
of the fifth grade.

They sent me to bounce around the prisons of Moscow.
In your
tiny little
apartment world,
bedroom lyrics grow up with soft curls.
What could anyone find in those lapdog poems?!
I, you see,
learned
to love
in Butyrki.
What's the Bois de Boulogne's languor to me?!
What use do I have for seascape sighs?!
I
fell in love
with the Office of Funeral Processions
through the peephole of cell 103.
They would look up at the sun every day
and get cocky:
"How much might those little rays be worth?"
Whereas I,
at that time,
for the yellow rabbit
on my wall,
would have given up everything in this world.

My University

You know French.
You can divide
and multiply.
You decline like a dream.
Go ahead and decline, then!
But tell me this—
can you

sing a duet with a building?
Do you understand the language of streetcars?
A human nestling,
the moment it hatches,
reaches for booklets,
for notebook pages.
Whereas I learned my ABCs from signboards,
leafing through pages of iron and tin.
They take the earth,
cut it down,
peel it;
and that's how they learn—
with a miniature globe.
Whereas I
couldn't help learning geography
with my haunches,
as I flopped down
to sleep on the ground every night!
Ilovaiskys are wracked by burning questions:
"Was Barbarossa's beard really red?"
Go ahead!
I don't root through dust-caked nonsense—
every bit of gossip in Moscow is known to me!
They pick up a Dobroliubov book to learn to hate evil,
but his very name is against it,
the whole family tree yipping in protest!
I
learned
as a child to hate the fat cats,
always selling
myself to get dinner.
They finish their learning
and take a seat;
in order to please some lady,

tiny thoughts jangle from their little brass foreheads.
Whereas I
only talked
to apartment buildings,
water-pump stations my only company.
Pricking up the ears of their dormer windows,
the rooftops would catch every word I let fall.
And later
they'd jabber
about the night
and one another,
wagging their weathervane tongues.

All Grown Up

Grown-ups have business,
their pockets full of rubles.
Love?
Right this way!
That'll be one hundred rubles.
Whereas I,
homeless,
stuffed
my giant hands
in my torn pockets
and moseyed around, wide-eyed.
Nighttime.
You put on your best clothes.
Have your way with wives and widows.
Whereas I
was smothered in Moscow's embrace
by the ring of its endless Sadovayas.
In your hearts,
in your little pocket watches,

mistresses tick and tock.
Your partners in the love bed are thrilled.
Whereas I listened to the wild heartbeat
of capitals,
lying down on Strastnaya Square.
Shirt all unbuttoned,
my heart almost on the outside,
I expose myself to the sun and to puddles.
Step right in with your passions!
Clamber on in with your loves!
From this moment I'm powerless to control my heart.
I know where the heart calls home in other people.
It's in the chest—as anyone can tell you!
In me, on the other hand,
anatomy's gone mad.
I'm one big solid heart,
buzzing all over.
Oh, how many of them are there,
springs alone,
stuffed into my inflamed chest over twenty years!
Their unspent burden is simply unbearable.
Unbearable not
like in a poem,
but literally.

What Came of It

Impossibly big,
unnecessarily big,
like a poet's delirious nightmare it loomed—
the lump of my heart expanded in mass:
a mass of love,
a mass of hatred.
Beneath the weight

my legs
took wobbly steps—
as you know,
I'm
pretty well built—
but even so,
I trailed along like my heart's appendage,
my broad shoulders bent out of shape.
I swelled up with the milk of verses
and couldn't pour myself out—
seemed pointless—I'd just fill up again.
I was worn out by lyrics—
the world's wet nurse,
a hyperbole
of Maupassant's original image.

I Call Out

I lifted it up like a strongman,
carried it around like an acrobat.
The way they call voters to a meeting,
the way villages
on fire
summon help with an alarm bell—
I called out:
"Well, here it is!
Here!
Come and get it!"
When they heard
such a hulk cry out,
then, without looking,
through the dust,
through the mud,
through the snow,

all the ladies
shot
like a rocket away from me:
"We'd like something a bit smaller,
maybe something like a tango."
I cannot carry,
yet I carry my burden.
I want to cast it off,
but I know
I won't do it!
The arches of my ribs couldn't hold back the thrust.
My rib cage was cracking from the strain.

You

You came along
and went straight to your work:
looking
past my roar
and past my size,
you simply saw a little boy.
You caught
and took away my heart
and simply
went off to play—
like a girl with a ball.
And for everyone else
it was like some kind of miracle—
every lady,
every girl stopped and stared:
"Love someone like that?
But he'll run away!
She must be a lion tamer.
She must be from the zoo!"

But I rejoiced.
It was gone—
the yoke!
Forgetting myself in my joy,
I skipped
and jumped like an Indian at a wedding,
I felt so happy,
so relieved.

It's Impossible

I couldn't do it alone—
couldn't carry a grand piano
(much less
a safe).
And if I can't handle a safe
or a piano,
how could I
carry my heart, if I were to take it back?
Bankers know:
"We're rich beyond measure.
Our pockets aren't big enough—
we stow our money in a safe."
My love
in you—
like riches in iron—
I hid,
and I walked around
rejoicing like Croesus.
And only
if someday I really wanted to,
I'd take out a smile,
a half-smile,
or less—

carousing with my friends,
I'd spend, one midnight,
about fifteen rubles of lyrical small change.

So It Was with Me

Naval fleets come together in harbor.
The train hurries back to its station.
How much more so with me, then—
after all, I'm in love!—
I am drawn and I bend toward you.
Pushkin's miserly knight descends
to admire and rummage in his cellar full of riches.
So I
return to you, beloved.
It's my own heart—
I'm admiring what's mine.
Coming home is a joyous occasion.
Scraping off the dirt,
shaving and washing.
That's just the way
I come back to you—
after all,
coming
to you,
am I not coming home?!
Everything earthly is received by the earth.
We all return to our final goal.
So I
reach
steadfastly for you,
the moment we part,
the moment I lose sight of you.

The Conclusion

Love won't be washed away
by quarrels
or miles.
It's been thought through,
verified,
tested.
Solemnly raising my line-fingered verse,
I swear—
I love
unchangingly and faithfully!

1922

Foreword

In The Truth
> *you'll find truth.*
>> *In* The News,
>>> *news.*

Facts.
> *You can lay them out*
>> *on the table.*

But a poet
> *is also interested*
>> *in what*
>>> *will be in two*

hundred years,
> *or even just a hundred,*
>> *maybe.*

I. The War Soon to Come

When
> we leaf through
>> newspaper pages

and ponder
> the news
>> from the quagmires abroad,

we come upon
> the inventions
>> of imperialist sages:

first gas,
> then rays,
>> then pilotless planes.

What are they,
                concerned for the chicken's bitter lot?
Do they harness their rays
                        to help
                                humankind?
Nope—
        they're just tossing down
                                a newfangled lariat
to loop
        round the necks
                        of the peasantry and proletariat.
For a decade now,
                death has stuffed
                                every page
of every newspaper—
                        mutilations,
                                horror stories.
And yet it will all seem
                        but a trifle,
                                today's carnage,
in the terror
        of future phantasmagorias.

. . . .

The Year 2125

The sky cupped its hands
                        to panhandle for stars.
It was evening,
                to say it plain.
In the sky,
        as always,
                there appeared a mini-airplane.

The usual kind—
                a skywriter—
                                for Aero-Rosta.
Moscow.
        The Muscovites
                    stepped out
on the roofs of their forty-story
                            commune-homes.
"Let's take a look, shall we.
                        What's it writing about?
Who?
      Whom?
            When?
                  To whom?"

Alarm

The pilot
        let rip
                the burning gas
and traced out
            in the sky
                a border.
Then he traced
            in giant letters:

                        | |
                        | ORDERS. |
                        | MOBILIZATION. |

                            And next,
                                  the telex:
R e p o r t.
            From the sentinels.
                      On the east coast.
We'll relay their update:

"At precisely
five minutes to eight,
despite
        the early hour,
the enemy
            snuffed out
                    their outermost beacon towers."
The sentinels sent up a flare.
                        In the dark were revealed
feverish preparations
            on the enemy airfield.
Wing to wing,
            wings upon wings,
their first,
        their second,
                their hundredth air squadron.
Another flare!
        Blazed.
            What did we see?
From the hangars
            they're wheeling out their destroyers.
"Encrypted for relay.
            Rebroadcast
to hundreds of Soviet
            sentinel posts.
Exemplary order.
        We're flying on a course
                    to intercept,
under cover
        of gas smokescreen."
Following the report,
            there came an appeal:
                    "Comrades,
                        it's clear!

A threat to Red Europe
                    and Red Asia
                                draws near!
America,
            the last haven of the defeated bourgeoisie,
is raising
            against us
                        its air force.
To hide
        in a hole
                    isn't the way of the working class.
Hands on the wheel!
                        Eyes on the gas!"
It seemed
            poison gas,
                        suffocating and deadly,
was already
            enveloping
                        millions of heads.
The people made haste.
                            Grabbed hold of their headsets.
Let fly at the radio:
                    "Pick up!
                                Hello!"
The motor fell silent
                    after barking out the distress call.
Up above,
            the phosphorescent light
                                died down.
The people
            wheeled out
                        their two-seater planes from the garage,

and flew off,
                    wives in tow,
                                    to the regional assembly.
Halfway
            there,
they were met
                    by people from central command.
Let's go!
            Let's go!!
                            Where the bombs and mines
are stacked
                in a frightening stockpile.

Radio Meeting

"Comrades!
            To the meeting!"
                                the radio screamed.
The masses
            rose up
                        like the sea in a storm.
And from Red Square
                        an octo-wing took off—
it was the mobile
                    Comintern field rostrum.
The scene
            will never
                        be forgotten.
In gas masks,
                in full anti-gas costume
the earth
            was laid out
                            like some fantastic scale-model.

And above,

        the chairman of the Comintern warned:

"Comrades!

        America

           on this day

compels the Union

        of Workers

           to war!"

And from Shanghai

        to the Irish coast,

           the phrases

skipped

        instantaneously

           along the radio waves.

Air Mobilization

Today

        you can forget

           about dreams and slumber.

The artificial

        sun

           at a billion candle-watts

was turned on,

        and from airport

           to airport,

shuttles

        of sleepless Muscovites

           hustle and bustle.

There were light recon planes

           and dreadnoughts of aluminum.

A worker knotted with muscles,

        anti-gas suit on,

fastened the hanging mines
                          and stuffed the voluminous
weapons bays
              full
                  of flying bombs.
Staff officers
              near the shuttles
                                formed into divisions.
They carved up the sky,
                        each marking his own
space.
        Then they made incisions
in the stars—
              the territories of dogfights to come.
Here's a pilot.
                A cluster of boys
                                  (with little-brother tagalongs)
is helping him
              get into
                      his helmet.
And he's explaining
                    to the Pioneers and Little Octobrists,
what's what
            and why all the fuss:
"We knocked them out of Europe,
                                out of Asia,
                                            but see,
they took to their heels
                        over there—
to America, that is.
                    In submarines.
                                    Overseas.

There
        they've got friends:
                        bourgooeys,
                                Coolidges.
Over here,
        we had forgotten
                all about them.
We're busy building factories.
                        Putting up smokestacks.
But they've
        been as busy as we.
                        They've got
                                chemistry.
They stink of gas,
                and they've been grinding their axes.
Well, now they've decided
                        it's about that time.
They've packed up their bombs.
                        Bombs the size of a city block.
They won't leave a single brick,
                        not a single leaflet,
standing.
        They'll beat us,
                if we don't beat them first."

Forward

One
        machine
                slips out of formation smoothly.
Flies down,
        has a look around.
                Well, what next?

Then it jerks up—
                    as if rejoicing—
and signals:
                    "This is your Commander in Chief.
I give the order:
                    It's time!
Forward!
                    Spin your propellers
                                        from here to Mars!"
They take off,
                    raising their megaphones.
And the air
                    thunders
                              with a cherished march.

March

The bourgooeys
                    mount in fury
up to the very
                    sky.
Comrade
          proletarian,
hop into your plane!
Beat it
          back home,
                    factory workers,
whistling through the clouds.
We are the flyboys
of the republic
                    of workers and peasants.
Where no cavalry
                    can ride,

where no foot
             can tread—
only
     the flyboy
                 can give chase
to the enemy birds.
Forward!
             Through the massive cloudbanks!
We fly
      on shining wing.
We are the flyboys
of the republic
                 of workers and peasants!
Measure
          yourself against the enemy,
painting the road
                   red with blood;
unto the very
               firmament
affirming
          our communal brotherhood.
Our flag
          will fly
                   among the stars,
giving
      workers
               strength.
We are the flyboys,
                    we are the flygirls,
of the workers and peasants!

The Beginning

At first,
      the recon planes
                 swung into a semicircle.
Then, behind recon
             came an arc of destroyers.
And behind them
           the gas-carriers
                 formed a line.
Clouds scattered
        at random
             from all the propellers.
And behind them,
        almost
             covering up the many-eyed,
headlight-teeming
           vault of heaven,
there flew,
        more enormous
             than dockyards,
hangars
      that could hold
             fifty planes at once.
When
     the turns
         were sharp,
at thousands of distinct
             pitches and pitchlets,
multitudes
        of repair planes
             roared
through the whistle-voice
            of their sirens and horns.

Right behind
            them
                        came the cargo transports,
masked
        by some kind of
                        gray mist.
And they're all so quiet,
                        not like some cart on the ground!
Arsenals,
            stockpiles
                        of medicine
                                    and food.
Beneath them
            the earth
                        arched like a little bowl.
People were waiting
                        in every
                                    paved concrete clearing.
The Lenin
            squadron
                        took off from near Minsk,
joined
        by the airborne residents of Smolensk.
Higher
        and higher
                        the pilots twisted.
High as can be,
                and then higher still.
The march no longer sounded.
                        The planes
                                    were like dots.
Down below—people squinted
                        and threw back their rooftops.

They checked.
Yes, we've got enough
oxygen and water.
Food
is served by a machine
in an instant.
And they climbed in,
having checked
all the wires and motors,
to the armor
of their gas-proof bunkers.
Join the defense!
The factories hum.
Cranes
lug giant mines past.
Escaping
underground from the enemy's gas,
Factory life
was on the lam.

The Campaign

They fly.
Birds
stare in wonder.
They fly.
Is that a propeller
or a star shining in the darkness?
They fly.
Way up high,
until
there's frost on the fuselage,
they fly.

Hardly able
            to keep up
                    with themselves,
                            they fly.
Speed
        works wonders
                    with the clock:
in the space
            of one day,
                    two full ones go by;
two suns
            in twenty-four hours;
and twice
            the moon rises.
And when
            they catch up with
                        the earth's rotation—
the eye
        leaps over
                a hundred places at once,
while the clock face
                    constantly
                            displays
one and the same
                motionless
                        hour.
They soar up,
            slicing through
                        the air.
Mouth agape
            in suffocation,
with difficulty
            they reach
                    with their weightless hands

to turn up the flow
                    of oxygen.
The recon planes
                    slice into
                              a storm,
                                        into thunder,
and then, snapping out
                    of their thunderous stupor,
shoot down
          to the ocean's smooth surface
                                        like a missile,
and hover there,
              churning the water into foam.
One plane gets blown up
                    by a floating
                                mine.
And at that moment,
                  all the rest
double-time it
            to escape underwater,
slamming shut
            their steel-plated armor.
They surface,
            having passed through the danger zone,
shaking
       drops of water
                    from their propellers;
and once again
            into the sky,
                        flaming and red,
they sprinkle
           the ellipses
                      of planes.
                              They fly.

Minutes . . .
         Days . . .
                  Weeks . . .
                           They fly.
Through scatterings of the sun,
                  through shoals of the moon,
                                    they fly.

The Enemy Attacks

The commander
                  calmly
                           shifts the leather
battle plan
         rolled up on its two
                           cylinders.
All is calm.
         And suddenly,
                  flat out of nowhere,
like a stone,
         comes an airplane.
Then there's nothing.
                  Only
                           a giant mega-ray
reaches out
         like an enormous
                           hand.
They rise up
         like mirages in the desert,
one hundred thousand
                  planes
                           of the enemy squadron.

Aiming
          their rays
                    of destruction,
from ten sides at once—
                         ten if it was one—
the monsters whistled,
                    flew,
                         and raced—
monsters of light,
               of steel,
                         of aluminum.
A current of air
               sent the planes
                              reeling,
and they banked
               sharply
                     to the left.
Across
     their right wing
                    three big *K*'s ran—
the three
        black
             K's
                 of the Ku Klux Klan.
Then the wind
             attacked from the other side,
rocking
       them all to the right,
and in black
           on their left wing
                             there appeared
a fascist
        flourish.

In a split second
                    they formed into a wild tornado
and were gone.
                    They disappeared,
                                        cloaked in gas.
In every aero,
                    from every side,
like
      a spark
                    in a gas tank,
two words
            ignited the heart:
                                    "Danger!
Enemy!"

The Air Battle

There was no discerning
                            the blurred horizon.
Sky,
      air,
            water,
                    all in one!
And in this
            blue haze,
                            the final battle raged.
The ultimate contest
                        of reds
                                and whites.
An unbelievable battle!
                            Not a single rumblette!!
No artillery,
            no bullets did I see whizzing by—

only
        the propellers'
                        frenzied mechanics,
nothing
            but
                rays and chemistry.
In hot pursuit,
                    our boys would get carried away by the chase
and suddenly
                turn
                    back around.
Their hands would dangle,
                            and in their
                                        purple faces,
their eyes, gone glassy,
                        would pop out from the gas.
The attacking
                squadrons
                            would bore through the clouds,
then our projector
                    would open
                                its round eye—
and suddenly there wouldn't be
                            any more squadrons.
Just scraps and coals
                    floating down
                                from the sky.
Sometimes,
            unseen
                    turret with turret
would meet,
            and that
                    you certainly could hear,

because they fought
                    the old-fashioned way,
                                        hand to hand,
two
    dreadnoughts
                    boarding each other in midair.
One is destroyed,
                    and immediately,
                                        an idyll:
defenseless
            as puppies,
the wrecked
                dreadnoughts are led
                                    into hangars
and riveted and repaired
                            right there
                                        in the air.
Four times
            in a nighttime
                            pockmarked by stars,
the smooth surfaces of days
                            were exchanged,
but still
        the fight grew
                        and expanded,
raging
        day after day.
As the fifth day
                was slowly dying
                                in battle,
the enemy
            withdrew for a moment.

And then
            a thousand
                        clearly visible and terrible
machines
            took off, coming straight toward us.
Attack!
        On your rays!!
                        But they kept right on flying.
Hit the gas!!!
                But gas too didn't faze them.
Indestructible,
                they advanced without pilots.
Destroying
            everything
                    in their path.

They Press On

The commander frowned.
                        It looked like the end!
Our man launched an attack,
                        flapped his propellers—
and then dropped
            like a fly,
                    crossing his little wings.
Our boys were in a bad way.
                        Our boys were retreating.
The enemy's work
            was tidy.
                    They shot down a solid ton
with no mutilations,
                no pain,
                        and no wounds.

Then a whole city
                    was swept away
                                    without any groans
by a ton
        of suffocating
                        gas vileness.
Dozens
        of capitals
                        were eaten away by the invisible
gas that spared
                no one and nothing.
Right up
        to Moscow
                        the planes of the enemy vanguard
advanced,
        as if it were a parade
                                or a demonstration.
Those who had hope
                    were now
                                called liars,
but our pilots,
                fulfilling their duty,
in spiral
        rings
            of airplanes
converged
        right above Moscow.
Spread
        across the entire
                        lap of the sky,
at top speed,
            working their inexorable
                                    machine lungs,

the enemy flew
                    and attacked unflinchingly.
Now they were just
                    three miles away,
                              then two.
News
      of inescapable clarity
flashed up
            in black-bordered bubbles.
The radio
            loudly
                    blared it out:
"The Revolution is in trouble!"
The horrible sound of gnashing
warped
            even the calmest of faces—
it was Moscow itself,
                        screwing shut the hatches
on its underground
                    dwellers.
Viewed
        from above,
                    it was sheer madness—
such crowds;
            they're retreating
in dirigibles
            to the Urals.
Grabbing
          their wives and children.
They grew larger
                  and multiplied
                              across the sky's calico,
the advancing
              machines that seemed like peas from a distance.

They're about to drop!
                    It's about to break out!
The gas-bombs
              are about
                      to rain down.
Well then,
          let's get ready
                        for a suffocating death.
Is it like us
            to bow our heads,
                            begging for mercy?
Strained to the limit
                    by the monstrous
                                    air force,
the Land of the Soviets
                      fell silent.

Victory

And suddenly—
            unbelievably!—
                          it was as if
                                      someone
yanked down
           all the enemy machines
                                  at once.
To the amazement
                of our half-emerged
                                    pilots,
the planes banked
                and crashed
                            to the ground.
Not daring to rejoice—
                      is it some kind of trick?

maybe they've descended
                              to approach over land?—
our motors
                 started chattering
                                    and moaning,
dashing
            to the scene of the accident.
They flew low,
                     nestling right up to the ground . . .
In the huge pit
                     torn up by the drones as they crashed,
scraps of aluminum
                     and nickel
                                    were all they found . . .
No tricks.
            It's for real. They're kaput.
Our pilots climbed out.
                              Their foreheads all wrinkles.
A thousand questions.
                     The answer
                                    is mute.
And only
            toward morning
                              the radio solved the riddle:
"New York calling.
                 Everyone!
                     Everyone!
                              Everyone!"

The Radio

The pilots
            of the first squadron
                              send their greetings

to the workers,
                    peasants,
                              and airborne cadres.
Let Moscow
              be illumined
at a million
              candlepower.
As of this minute,
                    wars are forever
over.
    We,
          a squadron of Muscovites,
broke through.
                    They
                          didn't see us.
We passed
              underwater to America.
Then we flew up.
                    At night
                              we set up
our loudspeakers,
                    and boomed out
                              all over New York:
"Workers!
          Comrades and brothers!
How long
          till this fog
                    of nations disperses?!
For what pieces of silver,
                              for what pay
did you
          your European brothers
                              betray?

Today
         they sic you on us:
                              'Get crackin'!
Envelop
         Europe
                  in a plague of gas!'
But tomorrow
                  the conqueror will be back
to slap
         his yoke
                  right back on your ass.
What's it to you,
                  this life
                           the bourgooeys gave you?
They squeeze it all
                  out of you—
                              now blood,
                                       now sweat.
Unite
      with us
            in one solidarity.
In one commune
               without slaves,
                              without masters!"
Policemen came—
                  send a fox to kill a fox—
on aerocycles.
                  Their projector beamed out . . .
In vain!
         Rocking back and forth through the air,
our loudspeakers
                  still boosted the voices
of the best
            orators of the Comintern.

Nothing doing!
           You can't tie it up
                     or take it away—
the radio.
We could see
           that New York
                  was in turmoil.
The workers came out,
                the police took to their heels.
It looked like
           the city
              was switching on its lights
as flag after flag
           flared up.
The mines they had prepared
                for us
they laid in under the mansions
                of billionaires.
Wrapping
           themselves
              in banners,
they stormed
           the American Arsenal.
Just as in Moscow
              centuries ago,
the October
           storm grew and grew.
They advanced,
             booming thunder
                  across city blocks,
and broke through
              the clever array
                of locks.

It was some kind of radio-fort.
They took down
the guard.
They attacked
and took one half—
now for the other!
For an hour
the fighting was hard.
Then they grabbed hold
of some kind of lever.
They tugged on it,
twisted it a bit,
and in an instant—
no, that's too much—
in less than an instant,
there was a noise like a howl
plucked from a thousand
giant strings!
And a thousand
flying monsters
crashed down outside Moscow.

Joy

In a giant "hooray" our shuddering
mouths still
wanted to roar
and roar to their fill—
while
all across the sky,
an enormous telegram
was traced out
by Radio-Rosta:

"Peace!
        The nations
                have finished their fighting.
Long live
        this minute!
The great
          American Federation
is joining
        the Union of Soviets!"
There wasn't a doubt
                in anyone's mind.
It was signed:
        "The American Revolutionary Committee."

The Return

In the morning,
        dots appeared
                in the west.
As they flew home,
        they
                and their march expanded:
"We are the flyboys
        of the republic
                of workers and peasants.
This was no idle
        flyby—
the sky's vault
        has been cleared.
Peasant!
        Proletarian!
Now lower your airplane!

The factory workers
        shot
          downward,
             whistling through the clouds.
We are the flyboys
        of the republic
            of workers and peasants!
Where no enemy
        cavalry
          can step,
nor bird,
     nor human foot,
our flyboy
      everywhere gives pursuit
to the forces of the enemy.
Our flag
     will fly among the stars,
giving workers strength.
We are the flygirls,
we are the flyboys
      of the workers and peasants."

II. Daily Life in the Future

The Way It Is Now

A room,
     of course,
         is no sprawling woodland.
It's not the place
       to hold picnics
          or battles.

But it's just
            not for me,
                        this damned housing allowance—
with my
        constitution,
                    how can I survive on six square feet?!
Old men,
            old women,
                        a lady with a pug,
children
        without number—
                    that's the population.
Why, it's not an apartment,
                    but an Eskimo
or Kirghiz
        fishing village!
A child
        is not quite the same as a puppy.
All day
        you're hard at work.
First he knocks you
                    off your feet
                            with a ball,
then
    he locks you up
                in the bathroom.
Between the piles of stuff
                are paths
                        more winding than those in the Crimea.
Even the meekest soul
                could fly into a rage
                            from the noise.

All day
      the bells ring
            like in a belfry.
En masse,
        all alone,
           long rings,
               short rings.
And for the privilege
          of this nest
             among the cages
                  and pickle jars,
where there isn't even
          room
            to stick out your lip,
you're out and about
         all day,
           waving away
              notices of eviction
with a union mandate
         or some paper from the Commission.
You come back
        late at night,
           worn out from the city,
your face is all dirty—
        it'd be nice to wash it off.
In the dark
      in the washroom,
             you get slapped in the face
by someone's
      underwear,
         artfully hung up to dry.
Br-r-r-r!

The fumes from the kitchen
                    make me sick.
                                    I squat on my haunches.
I sit
     on the windowsill
                    with my face to the vent.
I see
      in the skies—
                    the bustle of airplanes.
I press against
                the glass,
                            driven into the frame.
That's who
            should
                remodel anew
our
     dismal,
            sardine-tin life!

What Will Be

I envision some future year
                            brimming with zeroes.
The battlefield's
                thunder
                        will have long since died down.
In Moscow
            you'll find
                        neither alleys
                                    nor streets—
nothing but airports
                and giant apartment blocks.

The days to come
                      are dark
                            and unclear.
But
     as a joke,
I'll depict
             for you here
one day in the life
                    of a citizen of the future.

Morning

Eight o'clock.
               The polite
                         radio-alarm-clock starts beeping:
"Comrade—
             get up now,
                     if you're all done sleeping!
Your factory
            calls!
If you have
             no further orders
                       for the alarm clock,
I'll offer you
             my good-bye greetings!"
Half-asleep,
            but still
                 with businesslike verve,
the citizen
            gets a quick
                   electroshave.
In a minute
            his hair's done,
                   and lo and behold,

his cheeks are smoother
                    than citizen Venus de Milo's.
He pops in a plug
                and opens his mouth:
the electrobrush—
                    zap!—
                        has just shined up his teeth.
Not a single servant!
                    At the push of a button,
a bathtub,
            by itself,
                    splashes out beneath him.
It soaps him up
                first,
and then gets to it,
                    scrubbing and thrashing.
Another button,
                and right up to
                        the citizen's nose,
a tea tray
        delivers
                itself.
He gets dressed—
                    no jacket,
                        no pants;
No off-size
            narrow shirt
                    to pinch him.
At once
        he's arrayed
                    from his heels to his hands
in silk
        of ingenious cut and fashion.

Into the shoes—
                a pair of feet.
At the window—
                a courteous ring.
Right up
        to his bed
                    from the lap of the sky,
a winged postman
                flutters inside.
No tax writs,
            no eviction notices:
a letter from his beloved
                        and several from associates.
His son runs in,
                a healthy,
                            chubby little guy.
"I'm flying off to school—
                        good-bye!"
"But where's your brother Vanya?"
"He's
    in the garden,
                    fluttering around with his nanny."

To Work

He takes a seat in an elevator
                            right there
                                        in his room
and gets off on the rooftop
                        with its flowers abloom.
Holding its course
                to the workplace,

an airship
            edges
                    right up to the eaves.
Lost in thought
                    (not trying to swindle anyone),
the citizen
            tries to board
                        while the ship's still in motion.
Putting on
            their most polite faces,
the air patrol
                stops
                    the citizen.
They file no reports,
                    there's no jangling of fines;
only
    a few polite words
                    of reproach.
Leaning his head
            out of the gondola,
                            his voice changing tones,
the citizen calls out
            to a flying acquaintance:
"Comrade,
            what's your hurry?
                        Give it up!
Fly by
        with your wife
                    sometime
                        for a visit!
If you're free later,
                stop by for a half hour
to flutter around and maybe play
                        some aeroball!"

"Will do!" the friend answers.

"Won't you

join me now?

Take a seat,

there's a space here in my gondola!"

The citizen switches seats.

Fifteen minutes

and that's that—

he arrives

at his place of work.

Labor

It's a factory:

Central Air.

What they make, generally speaking,

is compressed

air

for interplanetary travel.

Pop a tiny cube

into a cockpit of any size,

and you can breathe for days—

fresh, pine-scented air.

In the same way,

ages and ages ago,

they'd make tasty broths

from Maggi cubes.

Similarly,

now they manufacture

from clouds

artificial sour cream

and milk.

Soon
        they'll forget
                        what to call cows.
You'll never
                milk
                        that much
                                from any cow's udder!
Here's another factory,
                        a forty-tiered complex.
Forty workers
                with ferocious zeal
                                disembark.
Clean as a whistle.
                        No soot,
                                no carbon black.
The elevator
                delivers
                        one person to each floor.
No noise,
        no crowds!
Just a keyboard—
                a bit like today's Underwood.
Work is great!
                It'd be easy regardless,
but here
        the radio even plays music
                                to help keep the beat.
Simply punch the letters
                        according to orders,
and all
        the rest
                is taken care of by motors.
Four hours
        fly by in a flash.

And everyone's
                got air,
                        got sour cream,
                                got milk.
No need to sit there bored
                like sleepy night owls.
The working day
                is just four hours long!
When it's over,
                you're fresh as a squirrel—
                                no, even fresher.
Hit the showers!
                And you're done—
                                and it's time for dinner!

Dinner

The citizen leaves work
                and sees some children.
                                He yells out,
                                        "Simmer
down, children! Where are you off to?
                                It's time for dinner!"
No kitchen,
                no tedious domestic bustle!
The cafeterias
                of the Food Commissariat
                                are airborne.
You show up
and sit down.
You get some grub
and eat it up.
If you want, take two;
if you want, take five—

to meet anyone's taste,
for every appetite.
The dishes
            are self-clearing.
                        You finish eating
                                    and you're off!
The citizen holds
                a radiophone
                            to his ear.
He growls out,
                as he plays with the children:
"Give me Chukhlomsky!
                        Is this the Chukhlomsky commune?
Please let me speak
                to Ivanov No. 10!"
"Which one is that?
                    The clean-shaven one?"
                                        "No.
                                    With a mustache!"
"Good day to you, friend!
                        How's it going?"
"I just
        now
            flew past the fence.
I'm grazing my herd.
What can I do for you?"
"What do you mean?!
                    It's been painfully long
since I saw you.
                Drop by
                        for an aeroball match."
"Will do!
        I'll tend the herd
                        for another hour

and glide down
                    sometime between five and six.
I may be late,
                but not by much.
The village
            gave me
                    a little job to do.
The grains
            are getting burnt up in this heat,
and I
        am in charge
                    of the artificial clouds.
I'll have
        to make it rain,
                        but without any hail.
Good-bye!"

Studies

Now's it's time
                for study.
                        In a minute
                                the citizen
arrives
        at the Dairy
                    Institute.
Comparing
            the latest
                    technical data,
he studies
            in the lab
                    the properties of sour cream.
Nowadays we have
                various categories of pastime.

Let's say,
        workers load trucks,
                whereas poetry
                        is for the spiritual elite.
But in the future
                there won't be
                        more esteemed jobs
                                and less . . .
From cobblers
        to milkmaids—
                they'll all be geniuses.

Play

An hour later
        the citizen's at home
                relaxing.
                        He's changed his clothes.
In place of his shirt,
                there's an athlete's uniform.
Up in his racing plane,
                fast as the wind,
he flies,
        grabbing hold
                of an enormous ball.
The sky is filled
        with dancing planes.
The figures of adults,
                the cute little figures of children.
Even the old men
        come out to play,
                forgetting their traditional apathy.
Reds against yellows.
                Side against side.

They throw down
                    the ball
                            from a monstrous
                                        height,
and you've got to fly up
                    and catch it in your net.
Speaking plainly,
                football
                        is a bore.
A pastime
        fit
            for the equine species.
Whereas this
            is perfect!
                    You don't wear out your shoes.
The ball
        won't ever
                bloody your nose.
Everyone does somersaults,
                        whether they have to
                                    or not;
they slide up behind you
                    and do loops.
Finally
        someone
            misses with his net.
And then you hear:
                "Ho-o-o-r-r-ay!
                            That's one point for us!"
Up,
    down,
        forward,
                backward—

they somersault all over
                    then slip away again.
No out-of-breath panting,
                    no wincing faces—
it's as if
        they weren't responsible workers,
                                but dolphins.
If rain should arrive
                together with its friend, wind,
they rise
        above the clouds
                    and keep tearing along.
When it gets dark,
                but no one yet wants
                            to quit playing,
they chase down the sun,
                    and it's daytime again.
Finally
        the citizen tires
                of the throwing
                        and catching.
He descends
            and flies in
                    the dining-room window.
A button.
        He presses it.
                    In comes the tea table.
His son recounts:
                "Today
                    by accident
I broke a wing.
            I climbed in with Petka,

otherwise
        I would have been late
                      to arithmetic.
We got a free hour
              (the lesson was canceled),
so Petka and I
        flew off
            to catch a comet.
A bi-i-i-i-i-g one!
           Must have been a mile long.
The two of us together
              could barely
                    hold onto its tail.
Then
     we let it go—
              it hurt to give up such a big one!
But we're not allowed
              to bring comets
                  to school."
His sister:
       "Today
           the wind
blew a ball of yarn
              ten thousand feet down.
We had to go after it
             and wind up the thread.
I got all
        tousled up
           by the wind."
The youngest
         is all
            absorbed in his work.
He sits
     and writes in his diary:

"Today
            in school
                        we had a practical lesson.
We had to find out
                        whether there is
                                    or isn't a God.
The way we see it,
                        religion is an opiate.
So we examined an image,
                        a photocopy of God.
And then
            with our teacher
                        we flew through the heavens.
To see for ourselves!
We inspected the sky
                        inside out,
                                    upside down.
Neither gods
            nor angels
                        were found."
Papa,
            so as not to waste
                        a single moment,
Listens to the radio
                        read out
                                    the pages of books.

Evening

A phone call.
                "Hello!
                        I didn't quite make out your name . . .

Ah!
    It's you!
               Hello, my love!
Right this second!
                  I'm on my way!
                         In five minutes flat
I'll leap the whole distance
                   across the sky.
It's beautiful weather
              for flying tonight.
Wait for me
           by our cloud
                 under the Great Bear.
Good-bye!"
He got in his plane,
              and the squares
                   and buildings
                           receded . . .
Cheek to cheek,
           waist to waist,
they flew three times
              across outer space.
Along the milky ways
               they followed a comet's arc,
with their airplane
             out in front
                   pulling them like a horse.
Open space!
            This is no
               Petrovsky Park,
where you're always
              rubbing against
                  couples' backsides.

As they ride,
the citizen tells his sweetie-pie
about the way things were
                        back in '25.
"Today
        I was listening
                    to some radiobooks.
I tell you,
        those sure weren't the days—
                            just petty little daylets.
Even if you could find a room to live in,
                        it wasn't so sweet.
You applied to the Housing Committee,
                        sent the taxman his payments.
Whereas this is paradise!
                Open space,
                        none too tight—
the whole wide universe!
Let's take another random example.
Back then,
        in the spring,
                they'd all drag themselves to the dacha.
Via
    railroad.
Puffing
        and crawling along bit by bit.
It's the same
            as standing a swallow
                        on its legs,
and making it walk
                by stepping
                        from foot to foot.
To turn,
        to cut through the forest—

impossible!
               You had to stick to the rails.
And then,
            in ancient times,
                        there were also
so-called
        automobiles.
Another—
           with due respect—
means of conveyance!
Through the air—
               can't do it.
Through the water—
                  impossible.
Through the forest—
               can't do it.
Through a building—
               no way.
Tell me, now,
           what kind of a machine is that?
The tires burst,
             it's just a heap
                     of troubles.
It couldn't even
           go as high
                as a streetlamp.
A split second
           and then it broke down.
Now if I want,
           I can dart to one side.
Try that
           with a steam engine!
                     The little Primus stove!

Nowadays,
         you pop on
                    a wing and some wheels,
and pick up and leave,
                    together
                              with your house.
And if you want
              to make a stop—
why, there's Vinnitsa,
                    and there's Nice.
Sick people
          back in those days
were prescribed
              sunbaths.
Even
    in the day,
              you'd just fold your arms
and wait
       for a ray
              to poke through the clouds.
Whereas now
           you can fly
                    even if you're at the North Pole.
Get yourself warm!
                Have at it!"
His beloved
           imagined our long-gone days,
while beneath them,
                  cities
                         and settlements
flew by
      in illumination—
such daily entertainments!

The radio station
                    of the Urals
belted out concerts
                    all across
                              Siberia.
The notes they tossed off
                    just for fun
would make all the world's Chaliapins
                              burst
                                   with envy.
And then,
          in a cinematographic passion,
across the clouds they project
                    mile-long mirages.
This is no
          Art Theater,
                    this is no Ars,
where, squeezed between tight walls,
                         you've got parterre and tiers.
From the earth
          clear up to Mars,
pick a spot and *become*
                    either tier
                              or parterre!
Finally—
          in the future,
                    this too will come to pass—
right
     across the sky
                    they hold dances.
Without stomping,
                    without kicking up dust,
graciously
          arching their wings,

they beat out
                a fantastic quadrille
while over the radio,
                        the quadrille's storm sings.
All around,
            there are millions
                            of flying tables.
Have a drink and cool off,
                        at the ring of a bell.
A soft drink, mind you;
                    from cobbler
                            to tailor,
no one
        can stand
                even the smell of liquor.
For the sick,
            one shot of vodka's the norm,
and even that
            is administered
                        under chloroform.
No one
        is nauseated
                by any kind of stanza.
I tell you, it's not life—
                    it's pure bliss!
But this I must relay,
to the sorrow
            of my comrade poets.
It's not like today,
                when they pour out
                            in their thousands
verses
        that make everyone queasy.

Here
     things are good!
                    No public debates,
not a single meeting—
               it's civilized!
At half past eleven
           the radio thunders:
"Citizens!
       This is a reminder:
              it's time for slumber!"
Whistling
      from the incredible speed,
leaving behind
       the bustle of the ball,
the citizen,
      performing
         a sharp turn,
flies straight home
       and into his bedroom window.
He gets out of the plane.
           Presses
           a button.
His airplane folds up
       and stands in the corner
            like an umbrella.
He speaks five words
     to his radio
         as he gets undressed:
"Alarm—
    tomorrow—
       half past seven!"
The satisfied citizen
     turns over
        on his side,

gives a yawn,
             and closes his eyes.
And so
      he spent
            every one of his days,
our citizen
      of the thirtieth century.

III. An Appeal

The date
      of winged
           days may not be near.
Not so soon
      will we shout out
           in joy:
              "They're here!"
But I,
     the agitator for future days,
will lead you
      one tiny step
         toward them today.
In order for you
      to become
         like the children of birds,
and relax
     in comfortable
        gondolas,
every day
     we burn
        into your eyes
the letters—
     O D V F.

So that you, at some bright,
                    joyful,
                              future hour
might move
          across the sky,
today
     our fliers
                crash to their deaths,
flopping down headfirst
                        on the Khodynka.
So that human life,
                    in ages
                            to come,
might blast
          like a rocket into the skies,
I myself,
         tiring out
                    evening after evening,
wrote
     these very
               lines.
Worker!
        Peasant!
                 Check by feel
that the heavens
                 belong to you
                                as well!
With all your one-hundred-thirty-millions' might,
intoxicate
          the world
                    with a desire
                                  for flight!
Enough
       crawling around like a troll!

We'll find ourselves
                        a nice place for a stroll!
Give us
        the sky!
We will sprinkle the heavens
                                with rye
and pour out some clouds
                            to water the grain.
Give us
        the sky!
Thrust
        the sharp knife of words
into
    the fairy tale of the future!
Give us
        the sky!

1925

Source Abbreviations

Numbers separated by a colon (e.g., 1:423) indicate volume and page of the Soviet Academy of Sciences edition of Mayakovsky's works: *Polnoe sobranie sochinenii v trinadtsati tomakh*, 13 vols. (Moscow: Gosudarstvennoe izdatel'stvo khudozhestvennoi literatury, 1955–61). The commentary to that edition was prepared by some of the best Soviet scholars of Mayakovsky, including Vasily Katanian, Zinovy Paperny, Nadezhda Reformatskaya, Varvara Arutchevaya, Alexander Fevralsky, and others. Other sources are identified by author's last name and page number, with full citations in the bibliography.

I Myself

Mayakovsky's taut and entertaining autobiography was first published in 1922, then revised and expanded in 1928 to address events in his life up to and including that year. It reads at times like a parody of the genre, stylized and not always reliable in terms of facts (the Russians have a saying—"to lie like a witness"), but at the very least it shows the poet as he wanted to present himself. This is Mayakovsky with his guard up—some of the entries are purely polemical in nature—but it still relates the basic contours of his full and interesting life.

Memory

5   *Burliuk*   David Burliuk (1882–1967) was a central organizational figure and a minor poet and artist in the Russian Futurist movement. We will hear more about him in the course of Mayakovsky's autobiography.

5   *some kind of "nobbles"*   It is not clear exactly what noblemen or what historical event, if any, the poet has in mind here.

The Main Thing

5   *or '93 . . . no earlier*   Mayakovsky was born on July 7, 1893. He became sensitive about his age as he got older, which may explain his coyness here, or he may have introduced the mock confusion for comic effect.

First Memory

6   *"alon zanfan de la two three four"* A corruption of the first line of the Marseillaise. The children couldn't understand the French words, so Mayakovsky's father gave the line a quasi-Russian ending (1:421).

Second Memory

6   *"You-jean-on-eggin"* Mayakovsky simply runs together the first and last names of Alexander Pushkin's most famous protagonist (i.e., he writes "Eugeneonegin"); the rendering here is meant to convey the child's misunderstanding with less phonetic ambiguity in English.

Bad Habits

7   *Once upon a time . . . mountains* Lines from "The Argument" by Mikhail Lermontov (1814–1841), who was known for writing about the Caucasus (1:421).

Studies

8   *various female cousins* Mayakovsky uses a neologism here, indicating female relatives of varying degrees of closeness (first and second cousins, etc.).

First Book

8   *The Chicken Farmer Agafia* A children's book by Klavdia Luka-shevich (1:421).

War with Japan

The Russo-Japanese War of 1904–1905 ended in disastrous and humiliating defeat for the Russians, and the resulting widespread dissatisfaction with the tsarist government helped bring about the Revolution of 1905.

Underground Literature

9   *Snap out of it . . . right now* From an anonymous song ("To the Soldier") popular in 1905 (1:422).

10   *otherwise . . . mommy* From the satirical poem "Like in Our Village," author unknown (ibid.).

1905

10   *the Rioni*   A major river running through Kutaisi in western Georgia.

10   *General Alikhanov had been killed*   In fact, General Alikhanov wasn't murdered until 1907, a year after Mayakovsky's family moved to Moscow. A General Gryaznov, however, was killed in Tbilisi in January 1906; Mayakovsky may have confused these two events, both of which received a good deal of press and popular attention (1:422).

10   *SRs in red . . . other colors*   SRs were members of the Socialist-Revolutionary Party, and SDs were Social Democrats.

Socialism

10   *The Stormy Petrel*   A publishing house that printed Social-Democratic literature (1:422).

10   *"The Erfurt Program"*   The program adopted by the Social Democratic Party of Germany at a congress in Erfurt in 1891.

11   *the lumpen proletariat*   In Marxist theory, the unorganized lower orders of society who aren't interested in revolution.

11   *Lassalle*   Ferdinand Lassalle (1825–1864), a German socialist activist.

11   *Demosthenes*   Greek statesman and renowned orator (384–322 B.C.E.). According to popular legend, he overcame a speech impediment by practicing oratory on the seashore with rocks in his mouth (1:422).

Reaction

11   *Bauman*   Nikolai Bauman (1873–1905), an important revolutionary figure and Bolshevik party member, was murdered in Moscow by a Black Hundred reactionary thug in late 1905. The Bolsheviks used his funeral to generate publicity for their cause, staging a large political demonstration (1:422).

1906

11   *I can't stand needles*   Mayakovsky also developed a phobia of germs and infection as a result of his father's death. Later in life he became known for his fastidious bathing (he carried a portable rubber bathtub with him when he traveled), and would

also produce propaganda posters for the People's Health Ministry exhorting citizens to practice good hygiene.

11   *Set off for Moscow*   Mayakovsky's father died on February 19, 1906, and the family moved to Moscow in July of that year (1:422).

Work

13   *Bohms . . . and all handicrafts*   Elisabeth Bohm (or Elizaveta Byom in Russian, 1843–1914) was a popular landscape painter. "Russian style" refers to a school of landscape painting sometimes associated with Bohm.

Gymnasium

13   *Anti-Dühring*   An important Marxist text written by Friedrich Engels, which defends Marx's conception of socialism against attacks by Eugen Dühring.

Reading

13   *Marx's "Preface"*   Marx's preface to *A Contribution to the Critique of Political Economy* (1859).

First Quasi-Poem

13   *Like Kirillov is now*   An attack on the minor Soviet poet Vladimir Kirillov (1890–1943).

The Party

14   *RSDLP (Bolsheviks)*   The Russian Social-Democratic Labor Party, which had split into Bolshevik and Menshevik factions at a party congress in 1903. Lenin led the Bolsheviks, who after the October Revolution of 1917 would become the Communist Party of the Soviet Union.

14   *Was tested . . . trade/industry*   This test should be understood simply as the first few assignments Mayakovsky carried out for the party (1:423).

14   *Comrade Konstantin*   Professional revolutionaries had code names, and this was Mayakovsky's.

Arrest

14   *Gruziny*   A region of Moscow.

14   *Sanin*   A novel by Mikhail Artsybashev (1878–1927) that caused quite a scandal and was widely decried as pornographic (1:423).

Third Arrest

15   *Koridze . . . Gerulaitis, and others* Mayakovsky's fellow revolutionaries.

15   *Taganka* A street in Moscow.

Eleven Months in Butyrki

15   *Bely, Balmont* Andrei Bely (1880–1934) and Konstantin Balmont (1867–1942) were leading poets of the Russian Symbolist movement. Bely's experiments with unusual verse layouts clearly influenced Mayakovsky, foreshadowing the staircase layout he would develop in 1923.

15   *snivelutionary* Mayakovsky's neologism in the original is formed using the *rev-* prefix, which was common in Soviet-era abbreviations.

16   *Turukhansk* A village in Siberia. Many political prisoners were exiled to such remote towns after they had served their prison terms.

The So-Called Dilemma

16   *out of the Stroganoff school* In 1908–1909 Mayakovsky had attended the Stroganoff Art and Technical school.

16   *"flung a pineapple into the heavens"* From Bely's poem "In the Mountains" (1:424). Mayakovsky again singles out Bely, this time for apparently sincere (if understated) praise.

The Beginnings of Mastery

17   *Zhukovsky* Stanislav Zhukovsky (1873–1944), an artist in whose Moscow studio Mayakovsky studied during the first half of 1910 (1:424).

17   *Kelin* Pyotr Kelin (1874–1946), another artist who helped Mayakovsky prepare for the entrance exams to the Moscow School of Painting, Sculpture, and Architecture (ibid.).

17   *Holbein* Hans Holbein the Younger (1497–1543). Dostoevsky wrote in *The Idiot* that Holbein's gruesome *Body of the Dead Christ in the Tomb* (1522) could make a man lose his faith.

17   *Sasha Chorny* Sasha Chorny or Sasha "The Black" (pen name of Alexander Glickberg, 1880–1932), a popular satirical poet.

Last School

17   *Worked on heads*   Practiced drawing portraits (1:424).

17   *Enrolled . . . trustworthiness*   Mayakovsky enrolled in the school in August 1911, after being rejected by a St. Petersburg school because of his record as a political subversive (ibid.).

17   *Larionov, Mashkov*   Mikhail Larionov (1881–1964) and Ilya Mashkov (1881–1944) were both expelled from the Moscow School of Painting, Sculpture, and Architecture in 1910 (ibid.).

17   *Revinstinct*   Another neologism formed using the *rev-* prefix.

In the Smoking Room

18   *Isle of the Dead*   A symphonic poem, Rachmaninoff's op. 29 (1908). The concert described took place on February 4, 1912 (1:424).

A Most Memorable Night

18   *Russian Futurism was born*   Mayakovsky is mythologizing. Russian Futurism was formally born in 1910, when the miscellany entitled *A Trap for Judges* (other translations are possible) was published. David Burliuk indeed took part in that initial publication (as did Vasily Kamensky and Velimir Khlebnikov—see notes to pages 20 and 21), but Mayakovsky did not.

And So Every Day

19   *"The crimson and white"*   The first words of Mayakovsky's first published poem, "Night," which appeared in the miscellany *A Slap in the Face to Public Taste* (see note to page 20).

The Wonderful Burliuk

19   *Novaya Mayachka . . . "Port" and other poems*   Novaya Mayachka is an estate in present-day Ukraine that belonged to Burliuk's father (1:425). "Port" is one of Mayakovsky's first poems.

The Slap

20   *Khlebnikov*   Victor Khlebnikov (1885–1922), who later adopted the ultra-Slavic given name Velimir, was one of the undisputed poetic geniuses of Russian Futurism, and a very eccentric character.

20   *Kruchenykh*   Alexei Kruchenykh (1886–1968) was something of a wild card whose written work blurred the lines between art, critical theory, and prank. He and Khlebnikov were the key figures in the invention of *zaum,* a "transrational" nonsense language.

20   *A Slap in the Face to Public Taste*   The manifesto and miscellany (with Mayakovsky's first two published poems, "Night" and "Morning") came out in December 1912.

The Natives Get Restless

20   *Jack of Diamonds*   The Jack of Diamonds was a group of avant-garde visual artists. The public debates Mayakovsky mentions here, held in 1912–13, were about new trends in the visual arts. Mayakovsky argued against the Jack of Diamonds painters, claiming they were too conservative (1:425).

Of Course

21   *expelled us from the school*   Burliuk and Mayakovsky were expelled from the school on February 21, 1914 (ibid.).

A Fun Year

21   *Kamensky*   Vasily Kamensky (1884–1961) was one of the first Russian aviators as well as a Futurist poet and artist. As mentioned in the note to page 18 (see note to "A Most Memorable Night"), Kamensky in fact joined the Futurist movement before Mayakovsky, though he missed the first several stops of their publicity tour.

21   *my tragedy*   The tragedy *Vladimir Mayakovsky* is one of Mayakovsky's most important early works, building off and intensifying the apocalyptic, messianic imagery of some of his first lyrics (e.g., the "Me" cycle). He directed and starred in the Luna Park production (playing the title role, of course).

Early 1914

21   *"The Cloud in Pants"*   Mayakovsky's first long poem, which he would finish later that year (see page 359).

War

22   *"War Is Declared"*   Mayakovsky's first poem on the First World War, and indeed his first poem concerned directly with current political events.

August

22   *I went to enlist . . . Colonel Model* Mayakovsky's enlistment is dated October 24, 1914, and he was turned down on November 12 because of his criminal record. Colonel Model headed the police organization that denied his application (1:425–26).

Winter

22   *"Ach . . . shut the newspapers' eyes"* From the 1914 poem "Mama and the Evening Murdered by the Germans."

May

22   *Won sixty-five rubles* In a card game. Mayakovsky had a lifelong obsession with gambling and games of chance—perhaps not as pathological and certainly not as self-destructive as Dostoevsky's, but an obsession nonetheless.

22   *Kuokkala:* A resort town on the Gulf of Finland, now part of Russia and renamed Repino after its most famous resident, the painter Ilya Repin (see below).

Kuokkala

22   *seven-acquaintance rotation (seven-field)* The play on words here is based on farming terminology—the two-field system, etc.

22   *On Sunday . . . Repin's grass* Kornei Chukovsky (1882–1969) was a critic and theorist of literature and the author of popular children's books, Nikolai Yevreinov (1879–1953) was an influential theater director and playwright associated with the Symbolist movement, and Ilya Repin (1844–1930) was perhaps the most famous living Russian painter (and a vegetarian).

22   *a seven-foot-tall Futurist* Mayakovsky exaggerates his height here, but he was a tall man—a fact oft noted by his friends and acquaintances, as well as by the poet himself.

23   *Mustamiaki* A popular spot for summer houses not far from Petrograd (as St. Petersburg was renamed during the war). Maxim Gorky lived there at the time (1:426).

23   *Maxim Gorky* Perhaps the most revered writer in Russia after Tolstoy's death, Maxim Gorky (1868–1936) also became a kind of figurehead and spokesperson for Soviet literature, though his relationship with the Bolshevik leadership was rather complicated.

The New Satyricon

23   *"Pondering the prospects of a meal," . . . The New Satyricon*   The quotation is from a humorous short story by Chekhov ("Complaints Book"). Mayakovsky's work for *The New Satyricon* came mostly in the form of satirical hymns to various abstractions or professions: "Hymn to Dinner," "Hymn to the Critic," "Hymn to the Scholar," etc.

A Most Joyful Date

23   *L. Y. and O. M. Brik*   Lily Yurievna Brik (1891–1978) would be the love of Mayakovsky's life and his muse throughout most of his career, and her husband Osip Maksimovich (1888–1945) was an influential critic and theorist who championed Mayakovsky's poetry and eventually served as a kind of literary manager for him.

Drafted

23   *blueprints of automobiles*   Mayakovsky was drafted on October 8, 1915 (1:426). Due in no small part to Gorky's connections and intervention, he was able to avoid the front lines and find a place in Petrograd's Automobile School doing technical drawings. He would continue to work there until the October Revolution of 1917.

23   *"The Backbone Flute"*   Mayakovsky's second long poem (after "The Cloud in Pants") and the first major work he dedicated to Lily Brik.

23   *Six whole whole pages of dots*   Dots were used to indicate material removed by the censors.

Soldier Blues

24   *"War and the Universe" . . . "Man"*   Two more long poems written by Mayakovsky around this time. As he implies here, "War and the Universe" is more of an ideological work (antiwar and socialist), whereas "Man" is more personal and lyrical.

1916

24   *The Chronicle*   A journal begun by Gorky in 1915. Most of the excerpts Mayakovsky tried to print were rejected by the censors.

February 26, 1917

24   *February 26, 1917*   The central date of the February Revolution, which overthrew the tsar and installed the Provisional Government. In this section, Mayakovsky's elliptical style creates real difficulties for comprehension. The Duma was a legislative body, and Mikhail Rodzianko was its chairman at this time. Pavel Miliukov was the leader of the Cadet party and an important figure in the Provisional Government, serving as minister of foreign affairs. Mayakovsky often attacked and satirized Miliukov in his poetry. Alexander Guchkov was the Provisional Government's minister of war and the navy, and in this capacity, he was ultimately in charge of the Automobile School where Mayakovsky served.

24   *"The Bolsheviks of Art"*   Mayakovsky gave a lecture with this title in Moscow on September 24, 1917 (1:426). Much of the poet's activity around the time of the revolutions of 1917 was geared toward securing a leadership role for himself and his Futurist cohorts in the new literary establishment.

August

24   *Kerensky*   Alexander Kerensky (1881–1970), second head of the Provisional Government and another frequent target of Mayakovsky's polemics.

24   *New Life*   A newspaper where Mayakovsky worked for a short time in 1917 (1:426).

24   *Mystery-Bouffe*   An experimental drama in verse on revolutionary themes, which Mayakovsky would finish and stage in 1918.

October

25   *the revolution*   The October Revolution, that is, wherein the Bolsheviks seized power and through which (eventually) the USSR was formed. The question of whether one accepted (i.e., thought legitimate, approved of, etc.) the Bolshevik Revolution was commonplace at the time, and Mayakovsky wanted to be clear in his unwavering support.

25   *Smolny*   A historic St. Petersburg building that served as Lenin's headquarters during and after the Bolshevik Revolution, until the government was moved to the Moscow Kremlin.

January

25   *Acted in the films myself*   Mayakovsky wrote and starred in three
short films in the first half of 1918: *Not for Money Born* (based
on Jack London's *Martin Eden*), *The Lady and the Hooligan,* and
Fettered by Film (1:426). He would write several more scenarios in
the course of his career, but most were never produced. Of those
that were, only a few scraps have survived.

1918

25   *The RSFSR*   The Russian Soviet Federative Socialist Republic,
largest of the Soviet republics.

25   *the Proletcult at Kschessinskaya's*   Proletcult (Proletarian Culture)
was a movement that sought to look after the proletariat's cul-
tural interests the way the Soviet government looked after its
economic and political interests. At this time the organization
was called the Society of Proletarian Arts, and it was housed in a
palace that had once belonged to the court ballerina Mathilde
Kschessinskaya (1:427).

October 25, 1918

25   *Finished the mystery*   Mayakovsky's revolutionary drama in verse,
Mystery-Bouffe.

25   *Meyerhold and Malevich*   Vsevolod Meyerhold (1874–1940) was a
brilliant avant-garde theater director and close associate of Maya-
kovsky's. Kazimir Malevich (1879–1935) was a pioneer in abstract
art who founded the Suprematist movement.

25   *Andreeva stopped at nothing*   Maria Andreeva (1868–1953), a one-
time actor who became part of Petrograd's literary-theatrical bu-
reaucracy. She was Maxim Gorky's common-law wife.

26   *Macbeths*   Mayakovsky often uses the plural as a linguistic form
of belittlement, undermining the individuality of various proper
nouns (usually foreign names).

1919

26   *comfut*   A literary organization bringing together Communists
and Futurists (1:427).

26   *Art of the Commune*   A weekly newspaper published for a brief
period (December 1918–March 1919) in Petrograd (ibid.).

26   *"150,000,000"*   Mayakovsky's first overtly propagandistic long poem, modeled on the Russian *bylina,* or folk epic. Its title referred to the approximate population of the Soviet Union at the time.

26   *Rosta*   The Russian Telegraph Agency, where Mayakovsky produced hundreds of propaganda posters on various themes. The posters are commonly referred to as "Rosta windows" because they were hung in the windows of empty stores during the Civil War. He worked at Rosta from October 1919 until January 1921 (1:427).

1920

26   *Printing . . . here*   "I Myself" was originally written for an early edition of Mayakovsky's collected works.

26   *Denikins were approaching*   Anton Denikin (1872–1947) was one of the foremost generals of the White Army in the Civil War and thus an important target of Mayakovsky's propaganda. Note the poet's characteristic use of the plural with a proper noun.

26   *Did about three thousand . . . captions*   These numbers may be exaggerated, but Mayakovsky did work extremely hard at Rosta. Only a few hundred of his posters have survived to the present day.

1921

26   *Lavinsky, Khrakovsky, and Kiseliov*   Avant-garde artists and associates of Mayakovsky's (Lavinsky would later work with him at Lef).

26   *Third Comintern Congress*   The Comintern, or Communist International, was an organization dedicated to promoting Communist revolutions worldwide. Its Third Congress was held in Moscow in the summer of 1921.

26   *The News*   The official news organ of the Soviet government, *Izvestiia.*

1922

27   *MAF*   The Moscow Association of Futurists. A number of Mayakovsky's books from this period were published there (1:427).

27   *Aseyev, Tretiakov*   Nikolai Aseyev (1889–1963), a poet, and Sergei Tretiakov (1892–1937), a playwright and theorist of literature, would become two of Mayakovsky's closest colleagues at Lef (see below).

27   *"The Fifth International"* Mayakovsky never finished this poem, but he did create other utopias in the long poem "The Flying Proletarian" (1925) and in his dramas of the late 1920s.

1923

27   *Lef* "The Left Front of the Arts," one of many literary factions active in the Soviet Union at the time. These groups waged furious polemical wars with one another for leading positions in the Soviet literary hierarchy. Lef never met with much popular or critical success, as Mayakovsky acknowledges later in this section. In all, Lef published seven journal issues from 1923 to 1925 before shutting down, and then started up again as New Lef in 1927. The group's theoretical position in favor of "tendentious realism" (meaning journalism, chronicles, and other nonfiction genres) and against fiction and fantasy became increasingly extreme and often seemed to be at odds with Mayakovsky's work as a poet.

27   *"About That"* Here the poet tries rather hard to make his poem fit Lef's theoretical criteria. It is a love poem, Mayakovsky's last great long poem devoted to "personal motifs."

27   *"Nowhere else but Mosselprom"* Mayakovsky is referring to his catchy, rhyming advertising jingles written for Mosselprom, a chain of food stores in Moscow. His description of such work as "poetry of the highest qualification" may be pure bluster or *épatage,* but as is frequently the case with him, it is difficult to tell.

1924

27   *"Monument . . . Kursk"* A poem commemorating the success of a mine in Kursk. Most of Mayakovsky's poetic output from around this time until his death consists essentially of versified Soviet propaganda.

28   *Traveled a lot abroad* Few Soviet writers were given permission to travel abroad; Mayakovsky was allowed because of his service to the state. While abroad, he acted quite consciously and explicitly as a representative of Soviet interests.

1925

28   *"Stroll Across . . . Yourself"* This collection was never published (1:428).

29   *that everything be based on names, on facts*   This theoretical obses-
      sion with fact, nonfiction, and journalism was the central tenet of
      Lef, and it became even more pronounced in New Lef.

1926

29   *Feuilletons*   A print-journalism genre that could be anything
      from fiction to criticism.
29   *Toured cities and gave readings*   Mayakovsky's talent as a showman
      and declaimer of his own verse was legendary. His readings were
      indeed quite popular, though perhaps more as controversial and
      frequently scandalous events than as artistic performances.

1927

29   *"Very Good" . . . like "The Cloud in Pants"*   In asserting a continuity
      between his earliest, lyrical long poem and his last completed
      one, which was overtly propagandistic, Mayakovsky challenges
      those among his contemporaries (not to mention later critics
      and readers) who bemoaned his abrupt career shift.
30   *"Conversation with Blok" . . .*   All these quotations are lines or
      sections from "Very Good."
30   *"The Universal Answer"*   Mayakovsky's readings usually included
      a question-and-answer portion during which the poet frequently
      had to face attacks from philistines and other ill-wishers. This he
      did with pleasure, wit, and, as a rule, success. At any rate, he was
      capable of outshouting just about anyone.

1928

30   *"Bad"*   Mayakovsky never got around to writing this poem and
      began working on satirical dramas instead. His most famous play,
      The Bedbug, premiered later in 1928.

The Early Years: 1912–1916

Night

Mayakovsky's first published poem already features the striking ur-
ban imagery and complex, composite point of view—a poetic version
of Cubist techniques in the visual arts—for which he would become
known.

Morning

In this companion piece to "Night"—the two poems appeared together in the same Futurist miscellany, making for a remarkable debut—the poet experiments with a highly unusual form of rhyme: he rhymes the end of one line with the beginning of the next. The rhymes he forms at the beginning of sentences tend to involve prepositions (which thus receive a stress they normally would not) and word fragments. In transliterated Russian (with stresses marked), the first seven lines read as follows: *"Ugriúmyi dozhd' skosíl glazá. / A zá / reshëtkoi / chëtkoi / zheléznoi mýsli provodóv—/ perína. / I na. . . ."* In the original, the poem is in fact bursting with rhyme—not only the unique beginning rhymes described here, but also traditional end rhymes and internal rhymes.

34 *yellow roses* Perhaps a reference to the "yellow ticket," a form of identification carried by prostitutes in nineteenth-century Russia.

From Street to Street

Mayakovsky later claimed this poem was composed during a street-car journey from Sukharev Tower to Sretenka in Moscow, which explains some (but by no means all) of its unusual, kinetic imagery. Its jarring rhythm and tortured word order have been preserved to an extent in translation, but at its core lies a kind of palindromic sound-play that cannot even be approximated in English. In transliterated Russian, for example, the first lines read: *"U- / litsa. / Litsa / u / dogov / go-dov / rez- / che. / Che- / rez , . . ."* The device's prominence fades after these opening lines—one can imagine the difficulty of sustaining such a feat over an entire poem—but it returns briefly in the middle (around the lines "We are conquered! / Baths. / Showers. / Elevator. / The bodice of the soul . . . ," which are otherwise inscrutable in English).

36 *Up in the sky a giraffe sketch is ready / to color its rusty bangs* A difficult passage, to be sure, but it has been interpreted as Mayakovsky's projection of himself over the cityscape he is observing: the poet sketched giraffes all the time, and he seems to have identified with the tall, awkwardly elegant creatures (Brown 79–80).

Could You?

One of Mayakovsky's signature pieces, which he performed at recitations throughout his career. At his last public performance before committing suicide, he explained to a hostile audience (they found his work unclear and obscene) that this poem should be immediately comprehensible to any worker. A tongue-in-cheek commentary, to be sure—the poem's imagery is defiantly opaque—but speaking more broadly, its message *is* straightforward: the poet turns the mindless routine of daily life (Mayakovsky's nemesis) on its ear and finds beauty where others cannot or will not.

Me

Mayakovsky's first poetic cycle, which was published as a lithographed pamphlet in May 1913. The poems were written out by hand and accompanied by Rorschach-like illustrations by the poet and his artist acquaintances. With a few exceptions, this is Mayakovsky at his most experimental and abstract—the imagery is complex and at times inscrutable. Nevertheless, the cycle introduces themes that recur throughout the early poetry: being abandoned by love, the poet's loneliness and obsessive empathy, shouldering the pain of other people, etc.

3. A Few Words About My Mama

40   *in motley peahens*   This may be a reference to the unusual costumes Mayakovsky wore at his early public performances (see "The Fop's Blouse").

41   *Shustov's factory*   A vodka and liquor distillery in Moscow.

41   *Avanzo's*   An art supply store on Kuznetsky Most, a major street in Moscow (1:430).

4. A Few Words About Me Myself

41   *I like to watch children die*   One of Mayakovsky's most controversial lines, which has given rise to all sorts of outlandish interpretations and accusations. I favor Bronislav Gorb's demystifying sexual reading: the poet is obliquely describing receiving oral sex at night beneath the walls of a cathedral, and the children he likes to watch die are his own *potential* children, or, not to put too fine a point on it, his semen during orgasm (Gorb 28–29).

Love

In this poem and the next, we see Mayakovsky's tendency to view everyday street scenes through a prism of fiery apocalypse, self-sacrifice, and ritualized violence, and his surprising ability to combine such imagery with endearing creative whimsy.

We

Sound-play of the type seen in "From Street to Street" is also used here, albeit less extensively: in transliterated Russian, the poem opens *"Lezem zemle . . . ,"* and "Road—horn of hell" is anagrammatic in the original (*"Doroga—rog ada"*).

The Giant Hell of the City

Yet another example of Mayakovsky's infernal urban imagery, this poem also demonstrates his affinity for augmentative and diminutive suffixes in Russian: "Giant Hell" is expressed in the title and first stanza of the original by adding the augmentative and sinister suffix *–ishche* to the word for hell. Also in the first stanza, on the other hand, the same word is altered with a diminutive suffix to express the idea of "minuscule hellikins" (a poor approximation).

Take That!

A strident expression of Mayakovsky's contempt for philistinism, and a prime example of his and his Futurist cohorts' attempts to scandalize the public and *épater les bourgeois*.

46   *the butterfly of the poet's heart* A reference to the large bow tie the poet frequently wore during his public performances as a Futurist.

They Don't Understand Anything

A humorous poem that may very well be based on a real-life prank on an unsuspecting barber, but the complaint of its title would haunt Mayakovsky throughout his career. His stance as a poet was paradoxical and perhaps a bit immature: he challenged everything the reading public thought they knew about poetry and then was offended when they didn't understand him.

47   *Clown!* Mayakovsky here uses a characteristic pun: the word translated as "clown" literally means red (i.e., red-haired), and though he was not a redhead, the poet often used it in reference to himself.

In a Motorcar

Another experiment, on a smaller scale, with the kinetic imagery and shifting perspective that permeate "From Street to Street," only this time the poet is in an automobile, not a streetcar.

The Fop's Blouse

Another piece of programmatic provocation intended to scandalize audiences at the Futurists' public readings, this poem references the billowing yellow blouse Mayakovsky wore for those early performances (see his description of it in "I Myself"). Mayakovsky was often described as a fop, and he paid meticulous attention to his appearance throughout his career.

49 *burring my r's:* Pronouncing his *r*'s in the French manner, that is—an affectation common at the time among the upper classes in Russia, where French was still widely spoken.

Listen Up!

Another favorite for public recitation, this is perhaps most essentially an anti-aesthetic poem, rejecting stars as a conventional poetic image. Of course, Mayakovsky also mocks the bourgeois public who have become hooked on such images, and he doesn't pass up the opportunity to take a dig at organized religion either.

But Be That as It May

One of the poet's most successful early lyrics, demonstrating again the apocalyptic side of his urban imagery, but also his disarming whimsy (in the priceless imagery of the final quatrain).

Petersburg Again

A succinct expression of the poet's anti-aestheticism, iconoclasm, and antipathy toward literary tradition (at least early in his career): in the final two lines, he bashes the moon (as a poetic cliché), God, and Tolstoy.

Mama and the Evening Killed by the Germans

An example of the broadly antiwar verse Mayakovsky produced immediately after the outbreak of the First World War.

55 *Kaunas* A major city in Lithuania, which Mayakovsky refers to by an older name, Kovna.

Violin and a Bit Nervously

A delightfully surprising, eccentric narrative that has its genesis in what the Russian Formalists called "enstrangement"(see introduction): the poet describes a musical performance using personification, making it strange and novel for the reader. This modernist device gives way gradually to an unlikely romance based primarily on grammatical gender—*violin* is a feminine noun in Russian, while the drum, helicon, and poet are all masculine.

56   *Kuznetsky*   Kuznetsky Most, a fashionable street in Moscow and the setting of more than one Mayakovsky poem.

56   *without tact:*   There is a pun in the original: the Russian word *takt* also has various music-related meanings—time, beat, measure, bar. Indeed, in the context of the poem, these meanings should perhaps take precedence, in which case the line could be translated "not in time" or "off the beat," etc.

56   *the helicon*   A large spiral bass tuba.

That's How I Became a Dog

Another manifestation of Mayakovsky's me-against-the-crowd ethos, filtered this time through the poet's love for animals in general and dogs in particular. Later in life, he would often sign letters to Lily Brik by drawing a picture of a puppy. One might also note the poem's characteristic progression from a simile in the opening verse paragraph to a realization of that device in the fantastical narrative that follows. The dog is first mentioned as the vehicle of a metaphor for the poet's anger, but it proceeds to run away with the poem.

58   *that barebrow moon's face*   One can compare Mayakovsky's neologism here to "goldilobe" (which might also be translated "goldenbrow") in the 1920 poem "An Extraordinary Adventure . . . ."

Lilichka! In Place of a Letter

Lily Brik (1891–1978) was the great love of Mayakovsky's life and his muse throughout most of his career, though the physical side of their affair was short-lived. She was married to Osip Brik, an important theorist of literature and close friend and ally to Mayakovsky. Mayakovsky lived with the Briks for much of his adult life, in an arrangement that raised a few eyebrows then and continues to do so now (according to Brik, her physical relationship with her husband had ended even before she met Mayakovsky). Brik relished her role as Mayakovsky's muse and provided him a great deal of emotional support through the years, but she admitted that she stopped loving him in a romantic sense relatively early in their relationship. Their interaction and her role in his work are extremely complex matters, but for Mayakovsky, this was very often an unhappy, obsessive, and oppressive sort of love. He seemed always to want more from her than she was able or willing to give. "Lilichka! In Place of a Letter," which was written during one of the poet's many quarrels with his muse, reflects this underlying dynamic.

60   *Kruchenykh's hell*   Alexei Kruchenykh (1886–1968) was perhaps the most radical of the Russian Futurists, half prankster and half experimental poet. He is best known as a coinventor and champion of "transrational verse" (*zaum*), which was poetry composed of semantically liberated phonemes (his most famous work begins "Dyr bul shchyl..."). In 1912, he published a long poem, coauthored by Velimir Khlebnikov, entitled *A Game in Hell.*

To His Beloved Self the Author Dedicates These Lines

Mayakovsky's brand of self-love turns out to be more paradoxical than a Zen koan. His gift for hyperbolic self-aggrandizement here collides with the pain of his oversized love, and the unstoppable colossus is rendered impotent and useless.

63   *"Caesar's unto Caesar, God's unto God"*   A truncated version of Christ's words in Matthew 22:21: "Render therefore unto Caesar the things which are Caesar's; and unto God the things that are God's." "Six words" in the first line refers to the quotation in the third line. In the original, the number of words is four, as Russian morphology allows for greater economy in the biblical reference (no prepositions are needed).

The Years of Upheaval: 1917–1920

Our March

Mayakovsky composed two marches in the years 1917–1918 (the other is called "Left March"). Both are at some level calls to arms, but they also feature difficult, elliptical sentence structure: like eighteenth-century Russian poets, Mayakovsky sought to win over his audience and readers by appealing to their emotions rather than their intellects. The poems' agitational impact is achieved through their overpowering and choppy rhythm, very much like a martial drumbeat or even, perhaps, a machine gun. Much of this effect, unfortunately, is lost in the English text, because Mayakovsky relies heavily on monosyllabic words that lose their brevity in translation.

67   *Our gold—ringing voices*   I kept the dashes in these lines to create a sense of staccato rhythm, but in the original they are standard stand-ins for the omitted verb "to be." Strictly speaking, then, the

lines should read: "Our weapon is our songs. / Our gold is our ringing voices."

67   *Great Bear*   The constellation Ursa Major.

Being Good to Horses

One of Mayakovsky's most famous poems. In some ways it is a straightforward narrative, and Mayakovsky's love for animals is well documented. Nevertheless, the poem is more often interpreted as a political allegory, a kind of pep talk to a country reeling from war and revolutions. It can also be read as the poet's pep talk to himself: Mayakovsky was in a funk in the spring of 1918, short on inspiration and writing very little poetry. However, this is no simple self-help poem, and one should not overlook the closing lines' essential ambiguity. There is one eyewitness account of Mayakovsky reading this poem at a private gathering in a subdued, funereal tone, becoming so despondent by the end that he had to step away for a time. Finally, the poem has an important literary subtext: cruelty to horses is a recurring theme in Russian literature, and Mayakovsky is clearly responding to a section from Nikolai Nekrasov's poetic cycle "On the Weather," as well as Raskolnikov's first dream in Dostoevsky's *Crime and Punishment*.

68   *Grip . . . Group*   I opted to transliterate, rather than translate, this onomatopoeic series, because I believe the sound-play to be central. For the record, however, the corresponding Russian words are "Mushroom. Pillage. Coffin. Crude."

68   *Kuznetsky*   See notes to "A Few Words About My Mama" and "Violin and a Bit Nervously." Kuznetsky Most—"Blacksmith Bridge," etymologically—was in one of the most fashionable regions of Moscow.

68   *to bell-bottom along*   Mayakovsky uses an ambiguous, neologistic construction here. A more literal rendering of the line would be "people who had come to flare their pants along Kuznetsky." Bell-bottoms were just coming into fashion at the time, and the overall thrust is that the gawkers are idly showing off their new pants along one of Moscow's main drags.

Ode to the Revolution

Yuri Tynianov was the first to see in Mayakovsky a reincarnation of eighteenth-century Russian masters of the ode, including Lomonosov and Trediakovsky (in a note to his classic essay "The Ode as an Oratorical Genre" ["Oda kak oratorskii zhanr"], 86). Indeed, Mayakovsky's decision to serve the Soviet state through poetry puts one in mind of the eighteenth-century system of court poetry and patronage. His unnatural, at times tortured sentence structure also recalls stylistic traits of eighteenth-century Russian poetry (see also introductory remarks to "Our March"). Mayakovsky's approach to state service, however, as well as the antireligious ideology of the state he served, lent themselves more readily to odic travesties or mock odes than to proper odes. In this poem one might note several travesties of the Christian *Gloria*, including the poet's final, blasphemous, *quadruple* blessing. Obvious as it may seem, this poem's ideological orientation cannot be taken for granted; it has in fact been interpreted as an antirevolutionary piece that satirizes the Bolsheviks' cruelty and predilection for merciless violence (Gorb 505).

70   *soared swearwords*   The English here is quite close to Mayakovsky's neologistic construction: he uses a nonexistent past participle of an intransitive verb (to soar) as if it were transitive: the idea is that the swearwords have been cast up into the sky, or "soared." Intransitive-transitive shifts were common in Mayakovsky's and other avant-garde Russian poetry.

70   *the Blessed : . . Kremlin*   St. Basil's Cathedral on Red Square in Moscow (the Cathedral of St. Basil "the Blessed") was damaged in shelling during the October Revolution (2:491).

70–71   *Glory . . . her dying voyage*   The Russian battleship *Slava* (*Glory*) was sunk by the Germans during the Battle of Moon Sound in the Baltic Sea on October 17, 1917 (ibid.).

71   *from the bridge in Helsingfors*   These lines reference a mutiny of Russian sailors against their officers in Helsinki (Helsingfors is the city's Swedish name) on the eve of the October Revolution (ibid.).

An Order to the Army of Art

This poem and the next two ("It's Too Early to Rejoice" and "The Poet Worker") appeared as front-page items in the weekly newspaper *Art of the Commune*. They represent Mayakovsky and the Futurists' attempt to seize a leadership role in the cultural hierarchy of Soviet Russia, so it is not surprising that Mayakovsky chose a military and proletarian idiom for his defense of the poet's profession. Neither Mayakovsky nor his Futurist allies would ever achieve much success or popularity among the Soviet leadership or the country at large, but that certainly didn't stop their polemics.

72   *R, Sha, Shcha*   The last two are the Russian letters ш and щ. One might note the overall hardness and Russianness of the letters Mayakovsky singles out.

72   *Sov-deps*   Councils (or Soviets) of Deputies. Various Soviet-era abbreviations and contractions played an increasingly prominent role in Mayakovsky's poetry after the Revolution.

It's Too Early to Rejoice

This poem represents the high point of Mayakovsky's "out with the old, in with the new" stance vis-à-vis the classics of art and literature—a feigned or at least exaggerated cultural illiteracy for which the Futurists were notorious—but it still feels more like a pose than a stance. Mayakovsky developed a far more comradely attitude toward his forebears in the 1920s. The strident military idiom of "An Order to the Army of Art" is here taken to an extreme—the front-page forum in *Art of the Commune* seems to have brought out the ringleader in Mayakovsky.

74   *Rastrelli*   Francesco Bartolomeo Rastrelli (1700–1771), an Italian-born Russian architect best known for designing the Winter Palace in St. Petersburg. Mayakovsky may have chosen his name in order to rhyme it with "shoot" (*rasstrelivai*), but he also mentions the Winter Palace later in the poem.

74   *Insurrection Square*   A reference to a monument to Alexander III in St. Petersburg (then Petrograd). The square had been re-named, but the monument remained.

75   *the Winter Palace*   The Petersburg home of the tsars (and the Hermitage), designed by Rastrelli.

The Poet Worker

Some of the comparisons Mayakovsky draws in this poem may seem simplistic, but the image of the poet as a vital part of the Soviet workforce is one he would cling to for the rest of his career (see the later "Conversation with a Taxman About Poetry"). The idea of the poet as a contributing and practically useful member of society was at odds with ingrained (largely Symbolist) notions of the artist as elite aesthete, high priest, or medium.

77   *with the water of their speeches*   There is a pun here that one encounters frequently in Mayakovsky's work. The Russian word for "water" carries the additional meaning of empty verbiage (calling to mind the common English expression "watered down," as in "watered-down writing," "watered-down speech," etc.).

An Extraordinary Adventure . . .

One of Mayakovsky's best-known poems, and another the poet often recited in public (there is a surviving audio recording of him reading it). It was written in the summer of 1920. Mayakovsky was living in Pushkino, a settlement of summer houses (dachas) not far from Moscow, and commuting to the city every day to work at Rosta (the Russian Telegraph Agency). There he wrote and illustrated propaganda posters on various themes, eventually producing over a thousand of them. The poem has been interpreted in many ways. Because of Mayakovsky's meticulous description of the setting (Pushkino), and because Alexander Pushkin was known as the "sun of Russian poetry" (or simply "our sun"), the poem could be seen as an allegorical settling of accounts with the national poet, something Mayakovsky would undertake more explicitly in 1924, in "Jubilee." There are also elements of the Don Juan legend present in the poem: a rash invitation to an imposing supernatural figure, the invitation accepted, and even the sun's bass voice (recalling the Commendatore from Mozart's *Don Giovanni*)—but of course Mayakovsky saves the day, and a tense situation fraught with potential tragedy is resolved simply and comically. By the end of the poem, the speaker is stridently optimistic and filled with a new resolve.

79   *goldilobe*   "Goldenbrow" is another possible rendering of Mayakovsky's neologism. A reference to Apollo may be intended.

80   *there flowed a strange lume*   The benevolent ether emanating from the sun is described using an elegant neologism suggesting clarity, lucidity, and brightness. Mayakovsky first used the word in the long poem "150,000,000."

The Soviet Years: 1922–1930

All Meetinged Out

As every Soviet edition of this poem gleefully points out, Lenin expressed strong approval of its antibureaucratic message (4:419). In the same speech, however, Lenin stated clearly that he was not a fan of Mayakovsky's poetry (in fact, he hated it and favored the classics), and indeed, few if any Soviet leaders were. This is a crucial irony that bears repeating as we encounter more of Mayakovsky's political verse: though he self-consciously and methodically devoted himself to serving the new regime with his talent and hard work, no one in the upper echelons of power ever wanted or asked for his service. In this poem, we see him satirizing not only bureaucracy itself, but the language of bureaucracy—the complex labyrinth of Soviet abbreviations and compounds. There is also a realized metaphor, as the concept of being in two places at once is understood and envisioned with gruesome literality. The title of the poem is a one-word neologism in the original. Through prefixation and suffixation, Mayakovsky creates a past participle meaning "those who have meetinged through themselves" (or "meetinged themselves out," etc.).

85   *some to Main . . . some to Enlight*   Abbreviations commonly used in Soviet compound titles. This poem, again, is a send-up of Soviet bureaucratic language.

85   *the Theater Division and the Horse Breeders*   The Theater Division of the Central Political-Enlightenment Committee and the Central Horse-Breeding Administration of the People's Land Commissariat (4:420)—not the most likely partners for a joint session.

Schematic of Laughter

An unusual poem and a bit of an anachronism in Mayakovsky's poetic development—at this point in his career, it was rare for him to use such a traditional stanza layout. The poem first appeared along with cartoon drawings by Mayakovsky, with each stanza serving as a kind of caption. It was also rare at this time for Mayakovsky to write such an apolitical poem, but "Schematic" reveals his understanding of the bare mechanisms of poetic humor: the original features a heavy-handed, traditional meter (alternating iambic tetrameter and trimeter—the same meter he used in "An Extraordinary Adventure . . ."), as well as what he called "whip rhymes." The latter are rhymes in which the second cadence "cracks the whip" on the first, shortening its syllables and deflating it semantically. Some of Byron's most flamboyant rhymes—including the infamous "intellectual"–"henpeck'd you all" from *Don Juan*—are perhaps the best analogy from the English poetic tradition, but Mayakovsky generally placed the compound cadence first; that way, the single-word clincher two lines later really does break the back of the rhyme, to unique effect. The poem also follows a comic narrative arc, with another tense situation resolved into a harmless nonevent, concluding in an absurdly grandiose, odic finale. The title is anagrammatic in Russian: *"Skhema smekha."* This playful shuffling of letters suggests that analogous shifts on various levels will inform the poem's structure and narrative (Lotman 234).

88   *the Oka*   A river in central Russia and a major tributary of the Volga.

Jubilee

The jubilee in question is the hundred-and-twenty-fifth anniversary of Alexander Pushkin's birth, which was celebrated throughout the USSR in the summer of 1924. Mayakovsky may have planned this poem as something of an apology to Russia's national poet—whom he had thrown overboard from the ship of modernity as a Futurist iconoclast in 1912—but it would eventually become something wider in scope: a kind of state-of-the-union address on literary life in Soviet Russia. Indeed, the speaker seems at times to forget his companion and addressee—Moscow's celebrated Pushkin monument, dedicated in 1880—as he goes off on unpredictable tangents. He drags the statue off its pedestal in a kind of realized apostrophe, and the two set off on a tour of the city, but Mayakovsky's monologue quickly turns inward, then meanders all over the place. The language is often simultaneously colloquial (bordering on obscenity) and highly figurative (bordering on opacity): this is Mayakovsky at his comic, bombastic, melancholy, and avant-garde best.

91   *I'm now free . . . from posters*   Mayakovsky wrote and illustrated hundreds of propaganda posters and jingles for the new Soviet state in the early 1920s, but by this point in his career he had moved on to advertising for state-run stores and trusts.

91   *Like a mere pelt . . . sharp-clawed*   A reference to the 1923 long poem "About That," in which the poet appears as a bear.

91   *melancholishka*   Mayakovsky's neologistic diminutive, transliterated.

92   *A blue snout . . . Sug-Co-op*   Moscow's Sugar Co-op had dark-blue signs with orange lines radiating like sunbeams, and in the center a lump of sugar, which in Russian is called a head (6:496).

92–93   *Bring us some glasses! . . . assorted visas*   A difficult, ambiguous quatrain. The semantic clusters juxtaposed are overseas travel and alcohol. Mayakovsky omits a word (or more than one) at the end of the second line (following the preposition "from," which rhymes with "visas" in the Russian). Furthermore, the words "Red" and "White Star" appear in English in the original, so I thought it appropriate to set them apart graphically here. The Red Star and White Star were two transatlantic steamship lines, though of course other meanings of the terms may apply (the red star as a symbol of socialism, White Star as a brand of cider, etc.).

93   *Onegin's letter to Tatiana*   The last two lines of the quotation that
     follows are indeed from Onegin's letter to Tatiana in Pushkin's
     Eugene Onegin, but the opening is all Mayakovsky.

94   *May-ake your way south!*   Here I have tried to re-create a pun
     on the poet's name. A more literal rendering would be "Loom
     southward!"

94   *Vladim Vladimych*   A shortened form of Mayakovsky's name and
     patronymic, Vladimir Vladimirovich.

94   *two Executive Committee members in love*   Gossip, slander, and ro-
     mantic intrigue at the highest levels of government (the tsar's
     court) eventually led Pushkin to his fatal duel; in this somewhat
     inscrutable passage, Mayakovsky recasts these circumstances in
     Soviet terms.

95   *Nadson*   Semyon Nadson (1862–1887), a lyrical poet of a some-
     what pessimistic bent who was nevertheless fairly popular during
     his lifetime.

95   *relocated somewhere around X!*   In this section of the poem, Maya-
     kovsky is imagining his collected works standing in a library with
     Pushkin's. Nadson would be between them on the shelves (as in
     the alphabet), but Mayakovsky envisions sending him toward the
     end of the alphabet. The Cyrillic letter he gives is щ (*shcha*).

96   *Kolya Nekrasov*   Nikolai Nekrasov (1821–1878), the most civic-
     minded Russian poet of the nineteenth century and a favorite
     of Dostoevsky's. Doctrinaire Soviet criticism shares Mayakovsky's
     high opinion of him, though for less flippant reasons. Instead of
     referring to him by name and patronymic (Nikolai Alekseyevich),
     Mayakovsky uses diminutives of both Nekrasov and his father's
     given names.

96   *Dorogoichenko . . . tEDious panorama!*   Here I have attempted to
     re-create another of Mayakovsky's neologisms: he modifies the
     standard word for "tedious" or "dull" to suggest the Department
     of Education, underlining the didacticism of the minor poets
     listed in the previous line.

96   *Yesenin*   Sergei Yesenin (1895–1925), a popular leader of the
     Peasant Poets movement and something of a rival or foil to
     Mayakovsky.

97   *Poltava shtoff*   A shtoff is an old Russian unit of liquid measure-
     ment equivalent to about 1.2 liters, or a bottle of that capacity.
     The reference here is to a strong, probably home-brewed alco-

holic beverage. On Poltava's significance more generally, see note to page 98.

97   *Bezymensky*   Alexander Bezymensky (1898–1973), a minor Soviet poet associated with the Communist Youth (*Komsomol*) movement.

97   *Kolka Aseyev*   Nikolai Aseyev (1889–1963) was Mayakovsky's colleague and comrade-in-arms at *Lef* (see next note).

97   *Lef*   "The Left Front of the Arts," Mayakovsky and his circle's literary journal from 1923 to 1925. There were constant polemics and infighting among various Soviet literary factions in the mid-1920s.

98   *make Poltava seem silly*   In 1709 Peter the Great defeated an army of Swedes in the battle of Poltava, about which Pushkin wrote a long narrative poem.

98   *Some Geezer-brained Pliushkin*   Pliushkin is a character in Gogol's *Dead Souls* who embodies extreme, pathological miserliness and spiritual death.

98   *That Negro!*   Pushkin's great-grandfather, Abram Petrovich Gannibal (1696–1781), was an Ethiopian prince. Peter the Great eventually took Gannibal under his wing and brought him to the Russian court. Pushkin was proud of his African heritage.

98   *Derzhavin*   Gavrila Derzhavin (1743–1816), perhaps the greatest Russian poet before Pushkin.

99   *d'Anthès*   Georges-Charles de Heeckeren d'Anthès (1812–1895), a French baron, mortally wounded Pushkin in a pistol duel on January 27, 1837. He is one of the most reviled figures in Russian literary history.

99   *a slave to honor . . . struck down*   Here Mayakovsky quotes Mikhail Lermontov's "The Death of a Poet" (1837), which scathingly and scandalously blamed Pushkin's death on Russian courtiers.

100   *Tverskoy Boulevard*   The street in Moscow where the Pushkin monument was situated in Mayakovsky's day (in 1949, the monument was moved from Tverskoy to the center of Pushkin Square; 6:496).

Tamara and the Demon

One of Mayakovsky's better known and more amusing metapoetic works, inspired by his journey through the Caucasus in the summer of 1924.

His concrete source texts are two works by the quintessential Russian Romantic poet, Mikhail Lermontov (1814–1841). Lermontov's short ballad "Tamara" (1841) recounts the legend of a Georgian queen who lured travelers to her tower by singing, granted them one night of wild passion, then beheaded them and tossed their bodies into the Terek: the price of the queen's love was death. In Lermontov's long narrative poem *The Demon* (completed in 1841), on the other hand, it is the love of the immortal and cursed title character that causes the death of the young heroine (also named Tamara, but not a queen). In Mayakovsky's version, which combines the titles and some of the characters of Lermontov's poems, no one dies, and by the end of the poem, the irrepressible speaker has apparently domesticated the fearsome queen.

101 *the Terek* A major river in the northern Caucasus that flows through Russia and Georgia into the Caspian Sea. The Terek figures prominently in both Lermontov source texts mentioned in the introductory remarks to the poem.

101 *Yesenin in a police station* In the 1920s, as his alcoholism raged out of control, Yesenin became internationally known for brawls and other scandalous behavior in public.

101 *Lunacharsky* Anatoly Lunacharsky (1875–1933) was the Soviet Union's first Commissar of Enlightenment and a frequent polemical target of Mayakovsky's, though he championed the poet's work to an extent.

102 *Peter Semionych Kogan* Kogan (1872–1932) was a critic and president of the State Academy of the Arts. Mayakovsky often mentions him in his poetry of the 1920s, usually putting his name in a rhyming position (see also "To Sergei Yesenin").

102 *Red Grain Fields* A Soviet literary journal published from 1923 to 1931. The name of the journal, however, is singular (*Red Grain Field*), which suggests that Mayakovsky is also rejecting Russia's flat agricultural landscapes (the Russian steppe, etc.) in favor of wild Caucasian vistas.

103 *Berdan* An American-made rifle used by the Russian military from 1869 to 1891 (and later, as a reserve issue).

105 *Let Pasternak write about it* Pasternak's book of poems *My Sister Life* (1922) is dedicated to Lermontov and opens with the poem "In Memory of the Demon."

A Farewell

Paris, Mayakovsky's 1924–1925 cycle of poems inspired by his travels in France, can be compared to his more substantial cycle about America (see the next few selections): one finds the same mix of boilerplate propaganda and more interesting personal impressions. In this, the final poem of the cycle, Mayakovsky expresses genuine admiration for and emotional attachment to the French capital. Its closing has given rise to the theory that Mayakovsky wished to emigrate to Paris—and that his final line is a veiled lament that the Soviet authorities wouldn't let him (indeed, they almost certainly would not have)—but this idea is difficult to support.

Shallow Philosophy over the Depths

In the summer of 1925, Mayakovsky crossed the Atlantic on his way to Cuba, Mexico, and the United States. This poem, one of the first in the cycle dedicated to the trip (*Poems About America*—see the next two selections), speaks to his boredom and discomfort during the long journey by ship. Its title already draws attention to the poem's central opposition—that of shallowness to depth. The depth and power of the ocean (both literally and as a symbol) are consistently and incongruously paired with the pettiness and triviality of the poet's musings; he seems to be mocking the traditional grandeur and drama of his environment. The idea of superficiality is also contained in the title: the ship and the poet aboard it are just skimming the ocean's surface ("over the depths"). This idea is reinforced formally in the poem by the very short, snappy closing lines of each quatrain: they represent a refusal on the part of the poet to delve deeper than casual, superficial remarks on his surroundings—and on the various contemporaries and current events that drift into his idle mind.

108 *if not Tolstoy, then a fatty* A very simple, "shallow" play on words produces the substantivized adjective "fat" by shifting the stress on Tolstoy's name back one syllable (*tólstogo* instead of *Tolstógo*).

108 *Only water* Another of the poem's leitmotifs is introduced by this micro-line. "Water" in Russian also carries the meaning "empty verbiage" (as in English we speak of "watered-down" speech or writing), so here the poet is not only providing a pithy answer to his rhetorical question in line three—water has never "played the philosopher"—but also suggesting that all that philosophizing is just empty words.

108   *Everything flows, everything changes*   These lines reference the
       panta rhei aphorism of Heraclitus: "Everything flows, and nothing
       remains still." The reference is understandable, of course, given
       the mention of philosophy in the first stanza, but Mayakovsky
       characteristically refuses to engage Heraclitus in any meaningful
       way—the aphorism represents an easy way out, putting an end to
       his musings on the ocean's change in temperament.

108   *Steklov's pen . . . water*   Yuri Steklov (1873–1941) was editor of the
       newspaper *Izvestiia* (*The News*) from 1917 to 1925. Mayakovsky
       held a very low opinion of his long-winded editorials, considering
       them to be the very worst of "watered-down" writing (7:472).

109   *she has neither bottom nor top*   Mayakovsky here uses an idiom that
       I have translated more or less literally. A more idiomatic render-
       ing might be: "she's sure down on her luck."

109   *It's like a fishy version of Bedny . . . the whale's are within*   Demian
       Bedny, or Demian "The Poor" (pseudonym of E. A. Pridvorov,
       1883–1945), was a party-line poet who produced antireligious
       satires, propaganda jingles, and versified journalism—in short,
       anything the Soviet regime required—written in a colloquial and
       catchy style. He was a large man who wore a mustache.

109   *where are the birdies?*   This closing line was something of an inside
       joke, as Lily Brik has explained: "Mayakovsky was keen on birds
       and bought up a bunch of them, of various kinds. He quickly
       grew tired of them and let them all go. One time Osip Maksi-
       movich Brik's father came over to eat and headed straight for the
       birds. They weren't there. A terribly surprised look came over
       his face, he turned to look at Mayakovsky and perplexedly asked
       him: 'Tell me, in essence, where are the birdies?' This question
       seemed to Mayakovsky extraordinarily amusing and full of deep
       meaning" (7:473).

Broadway

Mayakovsky was officially admitted to the United States as a commer-
cial artist (he made his living at this time writing advertising jingles for
Moscow stores and publishing houses), but he thought of himself and
was welcomed by various left-wing organizations as the "plenipotentiary
of Soviet poetry," a position that was made official in 1926 (Brown 272).
He toured workers' clubs and gave public readings, which were gen-
erally well received, though his audiences and reviewers were sympa-

thetic by design. He also worked constantly on new poems, poems that would eventually form the cycle *Poems About America*. It is an uneven cycle, with naive and ridiculous propaganda alternating with more accomplished, inspired work. The typical themes are rapture and awe at America's technological advances, coupled with haughty condescension toward its social and economic iniquities—a special Soviet kind of pride, as the poet describes it at the end of this poem. Personally, as we know from many letters he sent home, the poet felt a great deal of loneliness and above all boredom during his travels, problems which were no doubt exacerbated by his ignorance of foreign languages (he knew only Russian and some Georgian from his childhood). The few English phrases he did pick up frequently found their way into his poetry, where he relished the challenge of rhyming English with Russian and played other amusing macaronic games. "Broadway" is one of the more inventive and high-spirited examples of Mayakovsky's paradoxical blend of linguistic ingenuity and linguistic ignorance, though the effect is lost in translation: keep in mind that most of the rhymes in the original poem combine English and Russian.

113   *"Maxwell House coffee . . . drop"* Maxwell House's slogan at the time and for many decades to come.

The Brooklyn Bridge

Generally agreed to be the best poem of the American cycle, "The Brooklyn Bridge" expresses the poet's awe at a marvel of modern engineering and construction (the Brooklyn Bridge was at the time one of the longest bridges in the world). A fascination with technology and big-city life was common to many Russian Futurists, not to mention other modernist groups in Europe. Urban imagery was central to much of Mayakovsky's early poetry, though it tended toward the shockingly anti-aesthetic and apocalyptic. Here the poet offers up what is in essence an ode, complete with extended similes and an invocation of the muse (of sorts). The anticapitalist propaganda central to many other poems of the American cycle is almost entirely absent here, except in one quatrain toward the end, which Mayakovsky claims was added later in response to an objection shouted out at one of his public readings in New York (about the unemployed leaping to their deaths from the bridge).

115   *Coolidge* Calvin Coolidge was president of the United States from 1923 to 1929. As indicated by rhyme in the original and here, Mayakovsky mispronounces his name, placing the accent

on the second syllable. This kind of linguistic belittlement is a comic device Mayakovsky used frequently when writing of foreign leaders (including Woodrow Wilson and others).

120 *It's one hell of a thing!* There is a pun intended here. Mayakovsky often referred to his poems as "things," so one could read this final line as the future geologist's compliment to the poet on the poem he's just finished writing.

To Sergei Yesenin

A poem with a lengthy backstory. As explained in a few earlier notes (see "Jubilee" and "Tamara and the Demon"), Sergei Yesenin was a talented and very popular rival of Mayakovsky's—to this day his work is much more popular than Mayakovsky's, a fact only partially explained by the latter's ubiquity in Soviet school curricula. Yesenin was a leader of the Peasant Poets movement who wrote with great musicality on rural, agrarian themes; many of his poems were set to music and became popular songs. Toward the end of his life, he became a raging alcoholic. In 1922 he married the American dancer Isadora Duncan (his third wife) and went on a whirlwind tour of Europe and the United States, where he became known for his scandalous drunken behavior (fighting, trashing hotel rooms, etc.). The drinking eventually took its toll on Yesenin's mental health, and he suffered a complete breakdown in 1925. On December 27, after being released from a mental hospital for the holidays, Yesenin killed himself in dramatic and gruesome fashion in Leningrad's Hotel Angleterre: he slit his wrists, wrote a final, eight-line poem in his own blood, and then hanged himself. The closing lines of the poem read: "Good-bye, my friend, no handshake and no word, / Don't be sad, don't knit your brow—/ In this life, to die is nothing new, / But then, of course, to live isn't any newer." With the publication of this poem, Yesenin's death became, in Mayakovsky's words, a "literary fact." Mayakovsky believed Yesenin's death and suicide poem would push many people contemplating self-harm over the edge, and he resolved to write a poem to counteract this effect: as Mayakovsky saw it, this was a time to fight poetry with poetry. Of course, the crucial irony to bear in mind is that Mayakovsky himself was obsessed with suicide and would end his own life less than five years after Yesenin. Indeed, Mayakovsky's rejoinder to Yesenin's closing lines isn't exactly bursting with optimism.

122 *a lack of rapport* The word translated here as "rapport" was something of a signal word in the years immediately following

the Bolshevik Revolution, expressing the idea of a bond or union between the urban working class and the peasantry (7:492). Given Yesenin's status as a Peasant Poet, the critics' implication is that he never came to an understanding with his colleagues in the cities. Mayakovsky satirizes this simplistic notion.

122   *assigned to some union guy* The specific reference here is to the journal *On Guard,* the publishing organ of the Russian Association of Proletarian Writers (7:492). RAPP fancied its members the torchbearers for all literary development in the Soviet Union and may indeed have jumped at the opportunity to assimilate Yesenin.

123   *like Doronin—endless and tiresome* Ivan Doronin, a minor Soviet poet, had recently published a four-thousand-line poem entitled "The Tractor Plowman" (ibid.).

124–125   *they've already delivered . . . dedications* Mayakovsky was disgusted by the amount and quality of literature dedicated to Yesenin that came out immediately following his death (ibid.). He found such easy, automatic veneration to be bourgeois (as we know from "Jubilee"), but was also, perhaps, a tad jealous.

125   *Sobinov* Leonid Sobinov (1872–1934) was a famous Russian tenor who sang at a memorial event for Yesenin in January 1926 (there was a tiny birch tree on the stage). Mayakovsky thought the entire event to be in poor taste (7:492–93).

125   *"Not a word . . . not a s-i-i-i-gh"* This line bears some resemblance to a line from Yesenin's suicide poem (see introductory remarks to the poem), but is in fact from the Tchaikovsky Romance op. 6, no. 2, with words by the poet Alexei Pleshcheyev.

125   *with that Lohengrin* Sobinov was known for playing the title character in Wagner's opera *Lohengrin* (7:493).

125   *Kogan* P. S. Kogan (1872–1932), an influential critic whose name frequently found its way—usually in a rhyming position—into Mayakovsky's verse of the mid-1920s (in the original, the name is the rhyming word in this line). See also "Tamara and the Demon."

Conversation with a Taxman About Poetry

Another important metapoetic work, easier to follow and with fewer topical references than "Jubilee." The poem's comedy and novelty stem from the bathetic pairing of poetry with petty finance and the intersection of their respective vocabularies, but Mayakovsky was quite serious about the poet's active and essential role in Soviet society. In late August 1926, he submitted an official declaration to the tax authorities, demanding to be treated as a worker. Before the Bolshevik Revolution, Mayakovsky's attitude was broadly antiauthoritarian and antiestablishment, but afterward, he continually sought, and in fact, explicitly claimed a leadership role for himself and his allies in the new Soviet artistic arena. In other words, he switched from simply bashing the literary establishment to jockeying for position as a part of it. His actual successes in this area were quite limited, however, as his work was never popular among party leaders (nor among the workers to whom he paid so much lip service, who tended to find him incomprehensible or buffoonish).

128 *for failure to declare* Traders and various other professionals were required to provide yearly estimates (declarations) of their revenues, and those who didn't were fined. Mayakovsky officially protested this policy, explaining that it was extremely difficult for a poet to determine his expenses, what percentage of his earnings they represented, and so on. For this reason, instead of making the required declarations, he personally visited the tax inspector and detailed to him his various expenses and revenues (7:499). In other words, this poem is not nearly as fantastic as it might seem.

132 *You'll go through forty pounds of salt* Mayakovsky here refers to a Russian folk saying—to go through a *pood* (16.8 kg) of salt with someone means to know him or her well. Mayakovsky interprets the saying rather literally.

135 *the Bagdadi sky* Bagdadi is the village in Georgia where Mayakovsky was born and spent his early childhood.

135 *the cherry trees of Japan* Mayakovsky had planned to visit Japan on his way home from the United States in 1925 (thus making it a round-the-world trip), but decided to give up on the idea (7:499).

135 *all this debt collection* Here Mayakovsky plays on another folk saying. Another possible translation of the line would be: "But who needs all these just deserts anyway?"

136 *NKPS* The People's Commissariat of Railroads.

136 *knout* A whip used for corporal punishment in imperial Russia.

A Letter to Tatiana Yakovlev

Mayakovsky met Tatiana Yakovlev in Paris in the fall of 1928 and fell head-over-heels in love with her. Much has been written about their romance and correspondence—the latter continued until late 1929, when Yakovlev married Vicomte du Plessix, a French diplomat—and about the role Lily Brik may or may not have played in suppressing evidence (poetic and epistolary) of Mayakovsky's feelings for Yakovlev. This poem, for example, was published only in 1955, from a copy preserved by Yakovlev herself (Roman Jakobson obtained a facsimile). The campaign against Brik, however, seems to have been based largely on Russian and Soviet antisemitism—Yakovlev was ethnically Russian, while Brik and her husband were Jews. At any rate, Mayakovsky's affair with Yakovlev was in many ways a carbon copy of his unsuccessful relationships with Brik and other women he loved: the same obsessive, oppressive kind of love, the poet's insatiable need for affection and attention, and the same ultimate end (Yakovlev married another, much like Maria in "The Cloud in Pants"). Yakovlev does seem to have returned the poet's feelings to some extent—as she wrote, the intensity of his attachment was infectious—but she could never return to Russia as he wanted her to, and so their romance was essentially doomed from the start.

138   *my Republics*   The Union of Soviet Socialist Republics (USSR), that is.

139   *trains to Barcelona*   Yakovlev was planning a trip to Barcelona, where the famed singer Chaliapin was scheduled to appear—a situation which ignited the poet's jealousy (Brown 345).

140   *Viy*   A creature from Ukrainian folklore with enormous, long eyelids (Gogol wrote a story about it); if its eyelids are lifted up, anyone it fixes its gaze on dies.

140   *the patches on your shoulders*   A reference to Yakovlev's prior bout with tuberculosis, which had apparently left her body scarred (Brown 345).

Lines on a Soviet Passport

This poem, like many of Mayakovsky's political pieces, was later forced upon generations of Soviet schoolchildren. Its strident jingoism is naive enough to be almost endearing, but it seems to have been taken at face value by educational authorities in the wake of Stalin's 1935 enshrinement of the poet (like many of Mayakovsky's poses). As a result, it is one of Mayakovsky's most hated poems, though it is no less interesting in its execution—and no less filled with signature Mayakovskian devices—than his other patriotic and propagandistic verse.

142   *the double-sleeper English lion*   The word translated here as "double-sleeper" might describe a double bed, for example, or a two-person sleeping cabin on a train or ship. Mayakovsky combines this semantic cluster with a description of the coat of arms printed on British passports at the time (which, however, featured a lion and a unicorn rather than two lions). Some allusion to the proverb "Wake not the sleeping lion" (and by extension, its Russian counterpart, "Wake not the Russian bear") may also be intended.

144–45   *hammery, sickle-faced*   The colloquial suffix Mayakovsky adds to the nouns "hammer" and "sickle" in order to create these neologisms is generally used to indicate the unusual prominence of a facial feature or body part (forming adjectives like "big-nosed," "broad-chested," "ugly-faced," etc.), so he is implying that the symbols of the Soviet Union are a part of his physiognomy.

At the Top of My Voice

Here is what Mayakovsky had to say about this last-gasp cri de coeur, the only completed section of a planned long poem about the Five-Year Plan: "Very often lately those who are annoyed by my publicistic work say I've simply forgotten how to write poetry, and that posterity will take me to task for it. . . . I'm a man of decision—I prefer to talk this over with posterity myself, rather than wait and see what critics of the future have to say. For this reason I address posterity directly in my long poem called 'At the Top of My Voice'" (10:375). As indicated by the subtitle, what we have here is only one part of the introduction to this long poem. This is the civic-themed or political introduction, whereas the second introduction, represented by only a few fragments Mayakovsky was still working on when he committed suicide (see the next selections), was to be more lyrical, a throwback to his earlier love poetry.

146   *a certain boiled-water bard*   Mayakovsky's self-definition here is somewhat difficult to interpret. The key may be the poet's lifelong phobia of germs and pathological commitment to personal hygiene; he produced propaganda posters for the Health Ministry on the importance of regular bathing, washing fruits and vegetables, etc. On the significance of "water," see also notes to "The Poet Worker" and "Shallow Philosophy over the Depths."

147   *"I planted it . . . if you please"*   Lines from the Russian folk song "I Planted the Garden Myself" (10:375).

147 *curly-headed Mitreikins, levelheaded Kudreikins* Konstantin Mitrei-
kin and Anatoly Kudreiko were young poets starting their careers
at the time (10:376). Mayakovsky infantilizes and pluralizes their
names (part of an overall confounding of the two poets), hence
my adoption of the childish *-kins* suffix for Kudreiko too.

147 *"Tara-tina . . . trrrrrills"* These lines, an onomatopoeic represen-
tation of the sounds of a Gypsy guitar, are from a poem by Ilya
Selvinsky (1899–1968), a minor Soviet poet (10:376).

148 *some Yeseninized folk-hero crooner* Yesenin was a leader of the Peas-
ant Poets movement and Mayakovsky's frequent polemical tar-
get; see also "To Sergei Yesenin."

148 *numismatist* A coin collector.

151 *bourgooeys* My rendering of a (standard) colloquial and pejora-
tive word for bourgeois or capitalist.

152 *Lethe* In Greek mythology, the river in Hades whose water
makes the souls of the dead forget their lives on earth.

152 *FYP* The (First) Five-Year Plan, Stalin's blueprint to bring the
Soviet Union up to speed economically, mostly through rapid
industrialization and the forced collectivization of agriculture.
Mayakovsky uses a standard abbreviation, not an acronym, to re-
fer to the plan.

153 *C C C* The Central Control Commission (*Tsentral'naia Kon-
trol'naia Komissiia*), a Communist Party organ (10:376). The let-
ter names are spelled out in the original (i.e., Tse Ka Ka instead
of the acronym TsKK).

153 *my partisan booklets* Mayakovsky is punning on two meanings
of *party* as a relational adjective: instead of a Communist Party
membership card, he'll show all his party-dedicated, propagan-
distic (hence *partisan*) literature. Mayakovsky never rejoined the
party after his career as an adolescent revolutionary ended.

Unfinished Lyrics

These fragments from Mayakovsky's notebooks were apparently to be
part of the second, lyrical introduction to his long poem "At the Top of
My Voice." They represent a return to a style of love poetry Mayakovsky
hadn't written for a few years, but they are also imbued with an unchar-
acteristically quiet resignation. Though parts of the second fragment
may have been written as early as 1927, on the whole they speak to
the poet's mind-set during his final depression in the spring of 1930.

They were not published during his lifetime and are presented almost entirely without punctuation.

154   *a silver Oka*   The Oka is a major river in central Russia and a tributary of the Volga.

154   *lightning telegrams*   A reference to Mayakovsky's 1923 long poem "About That," which plays hyperbolically on the imagery of the poet-speaker sending "lightning telegrams" (a kind of fast telegram delivery service in Moscow) to his beloved, Lily Brik.

154   *as they say . . . against convention*   There is quite a bit going on in these two lines. First, Mayakovsky rearranges two letters in the official formula "the case is closed" to make it read "the case is peppered-out"; an approximate equivalent in English might be "the case is cloved." Second, the "love boat" is not only a metaphor for the poet's relationship troubles, but also a concrete reference to his office on the Lubyanka, which he referred to as a boat. Finally, the "convention" against which the love boat crashes (or runs aground) is Mayakovsky's old nemesis *byt*, a word which comprises many meanings: the daily grind, routine, conventional life, etc. The entire quatrain starting with "as they say . . ." is reproduced, with one important change, in the poet's suicide note (see next selection).

The Suicide Note

Mayakovsky shot himself in the heart on April 14, 1930, having written this note two days before. He was obsessed with suicide for most of his life, but several external stimuli may have pushed him over the edge, including a failed love affair (with Veronika Polonskaya), the poor public and critical reception of his retrospective exhibit "Twenty Years of Work," and his unhappy decision to leave his literary allies at Lef and join the Russian Association of Proletarian Writers (RAPP). It may be tempting to conclude that Mayakovsky had become disillusioned with the regime to which he had dedicated so much creative energy, but this view is difficult to support. Certainly he was disappointed with the Soviet literary establishment, which was becoming more and more conformist and doctrinaire. He and his avant-garde cohorts (the Futurists, Formalists, Lefists, and others) had clearly lost whatever leadership role they attempted to claim immediately following the Revolution, and before long they would all be mercilessly persecuted for deviating from the officially sanctioned aesthetic of Socialist Realism. Some believe Mayakovsky foresaw this development; conspiracy theorists even believe the poet to have been murdered by the secret police, though the evidence does not support this version. The definitive explanation of his death remains elusive, but this suicide note shows us one last flash of his creative consciousness in a perfect, if tragic, fusion of the poet's work and life. I have, for the most part, left his punctuation (or more often lack thereof) intact.

155   *Veronika Vitoldovna Polonskaya*   A young actor at the Moscow Art Theater with whom Mayakovsky was involved at the time of his death—relationship troubles were doubtless one factor motivating his suicide. Polonskaya was the last person to see the poet alive; he shot himself immediately after a heated argument with her.

155   *Give the poems I've started to the Briks*   Osip and Lily Brik (see introductory remarks to "Lilichka! In Place of a Letter") had long helped Mayakovsky edit his work and prepare it for publication. He thought of Lily as his muse, and Osip, an influential critic and theorist, tirelessly championed his work.

155   *As they say . . . misfortunes and offenses*   On this quatrain, see the last note to "Unfinished Lyrics." In the suicide note, the line "You and I are quits" is changed to "Life and I are quits."

155   *Comrades at RAPP*   Two months before his suicide, Mayakovsky joined the Russian Association of Proletarian Writers, a group he and his Lef circle had maligned and satirized in heated polemics. RAPP advocated a return to Tolstoyan realism. The decision was not a happy one for Mayakovsky—he more or less hated his "comrades at RAPP"—but a bitter and painful defeat.

156   *Tell Yermilov . . . we should have fought it out*   Yermilov was one of the more doctrinaire critics at RAPP who objected when Mayakovsky wanted to hang some agitational verse in the theater during a performance of his final play, *The Bathhouse;* Yermilov succeeded in getting the verse slogan, which mentioned him by name in an unflattering way, removed (13:354).

156   *2,000 rub. . . . to pay my taxes*   Two thousand rubles was no small sum at the time, and this addendum gave rise to off-color jokes— how could someone kill himself with that much money sitting in a drawer? The incongruous pairing of poetry and petty finance is reminiscent of the poem "Conversation with a Taxman About Poetry"; not many suicide notes express concern over taxes.

Selected Long Poems

The Cloud in Pants

Almost three years after he finished work on his first long poem, in the foreword to its first full and uncensored publication in 1918, Mayakovsky summarized the poem as follows: "I think of 'The Cloud in Pants' (censors crossed out its original name, 'The Thirteenth Apostle,' and I'm not restoring it here—I got used to the new one) as a catechism of today's art; 'Down with your love,' 'down with your art,' 'down with your social order,' 'down with your religion'—these are the four cries of the four parts" (1:441). Though this summary doesn't necessarily correspond to the content of the poem, it shows how Mayakovsky came to think of (or rationalize) his early work later, in more politically rigid years. The poem is a tour de force concentration of the lyrical themes and preoccupations of Mayakovsky's early poetry, with an emphasis on the poet's messianic role and his tremendous capacity for suffering. The love story it recounts is based primarily on the poet's brief romance with Maria Denisov, whom he met in Odessa during the Cubo-Futurists' tour of Russia in 1913 and 1914.

159   *A Tetraptych*   Though the censors made Mayakovsky throw out his original title, "The Thirteenth Apostle," he retained some of its sacrilege in this subtitle, which refers to a work consisting of four parts. The idea of a tetraptych, much like Mayakovsky's quadruple blessing at the end of "Ode to the Revolution," travesties Christian notions of the Holy Trinity and the significance of the number three.

1

162   *chimeras . . . from Notre Dame in Paris*   A reference to the Galerie des Chimères, a nineteenth-century addition to the medieval cathedral.

163   *Jack London . . . Gioconda*   Mayakovsky fancied himself a kind of Russian Jack London, and David Burliuk started calling Maria Denisov (see opening remarks to the poem) Gioconda, another name for Leonardo da Vinci's celebrated *Mona Lisa* portrait (Brown 118, 132). The two key names Jack London and Gioconda form an amusing rhyme in the original.

164   *And you were stolen*   The *Mona Lisa* was stolen from the Louvre in 1911 by Vincenzo Peruggia, an employee of the museum who believed the painting belonged in Italy. He was caught trying to sell it

to a Florence gallery two years later (one year before this poem was written), and the painting was eventually returned to the Louvre.

165   *his sisters, Lyuda and Olya*   The names of Mayakovsky's real-life sisters.

166   *Lusitania*   RMS *Lusitania* was a British ocean liner sunk by a German U-boat just off the coast of Ireland on May 7, 1915.

2

166   *nihil*   Latin for "nothing." One doesn't encounter much Latin in Mayakovsky's poetry; here the word rhymes with "books" (*knigi*).

168   *Krupps and little Kruppikins*   A reference to the Krupp family of German industrialists, best known for producing armaments, ammunition, and steel.

169   *golden-mouthed*   A calque of the Greek epithet *chrysostomos*, which was applied most famously to John Chrysostom, Archbishop of Constantinople (347–407), an important early leader of the Christian church.

169   *The present day's shoutlipped Zarathustra*   The Academy edition glosses this line as a reference to the ancient Iranian founder of Zoroastrianism (1:441), but Mayakovsky may be referring more specifically to Nietzsche, who also envisioned a new or different Zarathustra in his *Thus Spoke Zarathustra* (1883–1885).

170   *my Golgothas on the stages of Petrograd . . . and Kiev*   A reference to Mayakovsky's performances with his fellow Futurists during their tour of Russia. Golgotha, "the place of the skull," was the site of Christ's Crucifixion.

171   *the year '16 draws nigh*   Mayakovsky went back and changed his original line ("a certain year draws nigh") in 1918, i.e., after the Russian revolutions of 1917; "the year '17" would no doubt have seemed too exact a prophesy, but the poet wanted to appear a bit more clairvoyant than his original, vague prediction would have suggested (Brown 115).

171   *a thousand thousand Bastilles!*   The storming of the Bastille fortress and prison in Paris on July 14, 1789, was the flashpoint of the French Revolution.

3

172   *Burliuk . . . his own screaming-wide-open eye*   David Burliuk, Mayakovsky's friend, mentor, and fellow Cubo-Futurist, was blind in one eye.

173   *"Drink Van Houten's cocoa!"*   Here Mayakovsky references an incident that was widely discussed in the press at the time he was writing. A condemned man was hired to advertise Van Houten's cocoa with his last breath; in return, a large sum of money was paid to his family (1:442).

173   *a Bengal light*   A kind of firework.

173   *Severyanin*   Igor Severyanin (1887–1941) was the popular leader of the Ego-Futurist group of poets. He performed with Mayakovsky and the other Futurists at many of their public events, but they eventually had a falling-out, and Mayakovsky satirized his rival mercilessly.

174   *von Bismarck*   Otto von Bismarck (1815–1898), the conservative German statesman who presided over the unification of the German Empire.

175   *General Galliffet*   Gaston Alexandre Auguste, Marquis de Galliffet (1830–1909), a French general known for his cruel repression of the Paris Commune (a brief experiment with socialism) in 1871.

175   *Rothschild*   The Rothschild family established banking and finance houses all across Europe starting in the eighteenth century; their name became synonymous with wealth and luxury.

176   *like Mamai, its ass parked on top of the city*   A reference to Khan Mamai, leader of the Golden Horde in the late fourteenth century, though as the editors of the Academy edition point out, it was the soldiers of Genghis Khan, not Mamai, who sat down atop boards placed over their defeated enemies' bodies (1:442).

176   *black as the traitor Azef!*   Yevno Azef (1869–1918) was a double agent working for the Socialist-Revolutionary (SR) party and the imperial secret police. His name became synonymous with treachery and betrayal (1:442).

177   *Barabbas*   A criminal whom the crowd chose to free instead of Jesus of Nazareth (according to the Christian Gospels).

4

179   *Presnya's dirty hand*   Presnya is the street in Moscow where Mayakovsky lived at the time of writing (1:442).

181   *Tiana*   The heroine of an eponymous poem by Severyanin (ibid.).

182   *like Herodias . . . the Baptist's head*   Mayakovsky seems here to confuse Herodias with her daughter Salome, who is said to have danced around the severed head of John the Baptist (ibid.).

183   *Peter the Apostle*   Saint Peter the Apostle, or Simon Peter, is best known for denying Christ three times on the night of the latter's arrest (according to the Gospels).

183   *the Kickapoo*   A dance popular at the time (1:442).

183   *Sèvres-porcelain*   Porcelain from the famed factory in Sèvres, France, has long been prized for its quality.

The Backbone Flute

Mayakovsky's second long poem is his first major work dedicated to Lily Brik, who would be his muse for most of his career. It is quite characteristic, if paradoxical, that he depicts her as a demonic redhead loosed from hell to torment him: his love for her, though it would remain a powerful wellspring of creativity for him throughout his career, almost always seems to have caused him more pain than pleasure (with the possible exception of the period in late 1921 that inspired "I Love"). This relatively taut and carefully constructed poem is perhaps the ultimate expression of Mayakovsky's hyperbolic, bombastic, melodramatic, and tragicomic love.

1

185   *Hoffmann*   E. T. A. Hoffmann (1776–1822), a German Romantic author best known for fantasy and horror stories. This opening quatrain, which is repeated with a minor change at the end of the section, features outlandish, compound rhymes (e.g., *shagov mnu / Gofmanu*—Hoffmann's name in the dative completes an unexpected rhyme) prefiguring the "whip rhymes" used to comic effect in "Schematic of Laughter."

186   *Nevsky*   Nevsky Avenue, the famed main street of St. Petersburg.

2

189   *Gretchen*   The heroine of Goethe's *Faust*.

189   *Traviata*   Mayakovsky is referring to the title character of Verdi's opera *La Traviata* (the word means "fallen woman"), whose name is Violetta.

190   *the Strelka or the Sokolniki*   Popular places for horseback rides in St. Petersburg (Petrograd) and Moscow, respectively (1:443).

191   *Saint Helena*   The island in the Atlantic where Napoleon died in exile (1:443).

3

193   *elephants . . . sealed Pyrrhus's victory*   Greek King Pyrrhus of Epirus employed war elephants in the Battle of Asculum against the Romans in 279 B.C.E.

195   *Bialik*   Hayim Nahman Bialik (1873–1934), Ukrainian-born Jewish poet and pioneer of modern Hebrew verse. He emigrated to Germany after the Bolshevik Revolution.

195   *King Albert, surrendering all his cities*   Albert I (1875–1934) reigned as king of the Belgians from 1909 till his death. Belgium was subjected to harsh occupation by the Germans in the First World War.

150,000,000

Mayakovsky's first long poem written after the Bolshevik Revolution was conceived and composed during his time making propaganda posters for Rosta (the Russian Telegraph Agency). The poem, too, is overtly propagandistic, depicting the victory of Ivan, a conglomerate of millions of workers and forces of revolution, over Woodrow Wilson, the larger-than-life representative of all things capitalist and unjust. The poem's title is at least partly a response to Alexander Blok's long poem "The Twelve," which follows a group of twelve revolutionary thugs who turn out to be led by Jesus Christ; Mayakovsky's title is meant to suggest that the Bolshevik Revolution represented the will of one hundred fifty million people (i.e., the whole country), and not just twelve. Mayakovsky modeled his narrative on the *bylina,* a Russian folk-epic genre in which a simple underdog hero (often named Ivan) defeats—almost always with unexpected ease—an inconceivably powerful and dastardly enemy. Here, too, though Wilson and his America are absurdly built up into a preposterous, mechanized nightmare, Ivan's victory seems inevitable. Mayakovsky's caricature of the class enemy is characteristically energetic and inventive. Paradoxically, his description of Chicago, the den of bourgeois inequity and stronghold of the evil wizard Wilson, prefigures the aviation-based communist utopia he describes in "The Flying Proletarian." One might also note the poem's ludicrous geography: at times, Mayakovsky seems to suggest that Chicago is on the Pacific coast, and Ivan's journey from Russia to America takes him past the Dardanelles and Gibraltar before he finds "the lap of the Pacfic" spread out all aroud him. The end result of Mayakovsky's comic approach to his subject matter is that the ultimate battle between communism and capitalism degenerates into a professional wrestling match—"the championship of worldwide class struggle"—and the genre of the poem slips, whether intentionally or not, from epic to mock-epic. This apparent lack of seriousness enraged Lenin and disappointed Trotsky, who later provided a very interesting assessment of Mayakovsky as a writer and revolutionary. The poem was first published in the column layout Mayakovsky used for nearly all his work at the time, but he reapportioned the lines into the staircase layout for a 1924 edition.

197   *Browning*   A semiautomatic pistol.

197   *Vanka*   A diminutive of Ivan, a very common Russian name; this Vanka is anyone and no one (something like Joe Schmo), and should not be confused with the conglomerate entity Ivan who is the hero of the poem.

197   *Kerensky bucks*   Kerensky dollars were paper money issued by the Provisional Government after the February Revolution of 1917 (2:504).

198   *Wilson . . . you want a bucket of my blood?*   Wilson (1856–1924) was president of the United States from 1913 to 1921. Mayakovsky comically mispronounces his first and last names, stressing the second syllable of each, which leads to the belittling rhyme Woodrow / bucket (*Vudro/vedro*). He continues to play with the syllables of Wilson's name throughout the poem.

198   *Lloyd George*   David Lloyd George (1863–1945) was prime minister of the United Kingdom from 1916 to 1922 and leader of the Liberal Party from 1926 to 1931.

199   *treaty in Versailles*   The Treaty of Versailles, signed by Germany and the Entente Powers in 1919, officially ended the First World War.

200   *Tula, Astrakhan*   Russian provinces (and cities).

201   *Baku*   The capital of Azerbaijan, situated on the Caspian Sea.

202   *Who gives a damn about the saccharine trade?*   Sugar was unavailable during the Civil War, so a booming trade in sugar substitutes arose (2:505).

205   *Parabellum*   A kind of semiautomatic pistol.

207   *Volgas of love*   The Volga, the largest river in Europe, runs through central Russia.

209   *the Neva*   The major river running through St. Petersburg (then Petrograd).

209 *banyas* Russian bathhouses where people traditionally take steam baths and whip each other with birch twigs.

209 *Baarbeat . . . Ba-am-bam!* These lines feature sound-play around the Russian word for drum, *baraban* (used as both a noun and verb), and also the verb "to beat." The words *bar* and *banya* (from three lines up) are also echoed.

210 *The Council of Commissars* The Council of People's Commissars—the highest government authority in the Soviet Union (on paper, anyway) from 1917 to 1946.

213 *The Cheeple Strong Hotel* As will become clear, the America, Chicago, and Woodrow Wilson of this poem are almost entirely figments of Mayakovsky's imagination. Though he may have culled a few proper nouns from a travel guide, there was no Cheeple Strong Hotel in Chicago (nor was there a *Chipple* Strong Hotel, *Triple* Strong Hotel, etc.), and Wilson never lived in Chicago.

215 *Their number would make Khlestakov . . . gasp for breath* A reference to Gogol's 1836 play *The Government Inspector.* In the third act, as the main character, Khlestakov, is making up all sorts of lies about his glamorous life in St. Petersburg, he says the streets were filled with thirty-five thousand couriers coming to see him.

216 *Sukharev Tower* A Moscow landmark torn down by the Soviets in 1934.

217 *America's version of Onegin* Pushkin's novel in verse *Eugene Onegin* is written in fourteen-line stanzas somewhat similar in form to sonnets. The Russian word for "long johns" is another belittling rhyme pair for Wilson's mispronounced last name (*kal'sóny Vil'sóna*).

217 *Strausses* Interestingly, Mayakovsky's characteristically pluralized proper noun is justified here—Johann Strauss II (1825–1899) was known as "The Waltz King," but his father, Johann Strauss I, also composed waltzes and helped to popularize the genre. Indeed, the whole family wrote dance music.

218 *Adelina Patti* Adelina Patti (1843–1919), an Italian soprano, was one of the most celebrated divas in history.

218 *Whitman stands ready . . . unprecedented rhythm* Scholars have pointed out various affinities between Mayakovsky and Walt Whitman (1819–1892), including self-celebration and formal innovation (as Mayakovsky seems to recognize—"unprecedented rhythm").

218   *Chaliapin*   Fyodor Chaliapin (1873–1938) was one of the most famous opera singers of the twentieth century. Mayakovsky seems to have enjoyed the challenge of finding rhymes for Chaliapin (here he uses *v shliape,* "in a hat"). See also "The Flying Proletarian."

218   *Mechnikov*   Ilya Mechnikov (1845–1916), a Nobel Prize–winning Russian biologist and pioneer in the field of immunology. He also studied aging and longevity.

219   *école-des-beaux-arts*   School of Fine Arts (French). Written as one rather bizarre-looking word in the original.

219   *Longfellow*   Henry Wadsworth Longfellow (1807–1882), American poet and teacher.

219   *Clemenceaus*   Georges Clemenceau (1841–1929) was prime minister of France from 1906 to 1909 and again from 1917 to 1920, leading the country through most of the First World War.

222   *American Telegraph Agency*   Mayakovsky worked as a propagandist for Rosta, the Russian Telegraph Agency, at the time "150,000,000" was written.

224   *Arthur Krupp*   The Krupp family of German and Austrian industrialists ran steel and armaments factories in the early twentieth century; the Arthur Krupp Company (a cutlery factory) was located in Berndorf, Austria. See also "The Cloud in Pants."

224   *Creusot*   Le Creusot, a city in Burgundy, was a center of arms manufacturing in Mayakovsky's day (the Schneider company was founded and based there), but there was no prominent businessman or industrialist named Creusot.

225   *the Dardanelles*   A strait in northwestern Turkey. Its strategic importance—together with the Bosporus and the Sea of Marmara, it links the Mediterranean to the Black Sea—has made it a focus of ancient and modern wars.

225   *Kazbek*   A dormant volcano in the Caucasus.

226   *the morning lume*   The same neologism is used in "An Extraordinary Adventure . . . ." Mayakovsky's use of the word in this long poem, completed in March 1920, predates the shorter poem.

232   *the lines of the whole world's decadents*   Mayakovsky most likely had in mind the Russian Symbolist poets, who were sometimes referred to as decadent (often pejoratively).

238   *cinematograph*   An early motion-picture projector.

240   *spirochete . . . vibrio*   Types of bacteria. Spirochete is associated with syphilis, vibrio with cholera.

241 *Talmuddied* The Talmud is a central sacred text of Judaism comprising civil and religious law and legend; to judge from context, Mayakovsky's neologism is based on a view of the Talmud as a complex, arcane document likely to confuse people.

242 *mullahs* A title given to some Islamic clergy or to Muslim men schooled in Islamic theology and sacred law.

242 *Peter . . . his cathedral* Most likely a reference to Saint Peter and the Papal Basilica of St. Peter in the Vatican; the latter is a symbol of Catholicism and Christianity.

242 *With the bait of an academic ration we lured them* The years of civil war in Russia were hungry years for most people, and academics were given a bigger food ration than others. Mayakovsky himself applied for an academic ration in 1925 (13:192).

243 *Gorky, like a hen on her eggs . . . his worn-out authority* Maxim Gorky (1868–1936) indeed wielded enormous authority as a cultural icon of the Soviet Union, though his relationship with its leaders was a complicated one, and he spent much of his later life in exile. As a founder of Socialist Realism, which would later become sacrosanct in Soviet literature, Gorky represented much more classical tastes and styles than Mayakovsky and the Futurists.

243 *the Admiralty* A St. Petersburg (Petrograd) landmark and traditionally the headquarters of the Russian navy, the Admiralty is topped with a large gilded spire.

243 *Tsushima* The site of the humiliating and decisive defeat of the Russian Imperial Navy in the Russo-Japanese War of 1905.

I Love

Written between November 1921 and February 1922, this poem documents perhaps the happiest time of Mayakovsky's relationship with Lily Brik. His oppressive love and heavy heart (the latter a cliché he realizes in characteristically literal terms) seem inescapable at first, but Brik takes his heart away and plays with it as if it were a child's ball. The poem also recapitulates many themes from Mayakovsky's early lyrics—his uniqueness and separation from the crowd, his street smarts and life of adventure and mischief, and his rejection of the bourgeois conventions of art and love.

The Way It Usually Goes

248 *Müller* Jørgen Peter Müller (1866–1938), a Danish gymnastics educator who wrote a very popular book of exercises called *My System* (4:431).

As a Boy

249 *the Rioni* A river in western Georgia.

249 *Three Leaves* A card game (4:431).

249 *Kutaisi* A larger city near Mayakovsky's birthplace (Bagdadi) in Georgia. Kutaisi is situated on the banks of the Rioni.

As a Youth

250 *Butyrki* A prison in which Mayakovsky was incarcerated for eleven months, most of them in solitary confinement; see the "Third Arrest" and "Eleven Months in Butyrki" sections of "I Myself."

250 *Bois de Boulogne* The Bois de Boulogne is a large park on the western outskirts of Paris.

250 *Office of Funeral Processions* The building across the street from Mayakovsky's prison cell in Butyrki.

My University

250 *You decline like a dream* Russian is an inflected language, with nouns and modifiers that change their form (decline) based on their role in a given sentence.

251 *Ilovaiskys* D. I. Ilovaisky (1832–1920) was an author of popular history textbooks (4:431).

251 *"Was Barbarossa's beard really red?"* Frederick I Barbarossa (1122–1190) was a German Holy Roman Emperor whose nickname means "red beard" in Italian.

251 *Dobroliubov . . . yipping in protest* Nikolai Dobroliubov (1836–1861) was an influential critic and journalist whose name etymologically means "good-loving."

All Grown Up

252 *Sadovayas* The Sadovaya is a beltway road encircling Moscow.

253 *Strastnaya Square* A central square in Moscow now known as Pushkin Square. Etymologically, Strastnaya Square means "Passion Square."

What Came of It

254   *the world's wet nurse . . . Maupassant's original image* In Guy de Maupassant's 1881 story "Idyll," a full-grown stranger nurses from a young woman who is painfully lactating.

So It Was with Me

257   *Pushkin's miserly knight* A reference to Pushkin's little tragedy "The Miserly Knight" (1830).

The Flying Proletarian

This is one of Mayakovsky's most interesting long poems and one that blurs genre boundaries, containing propaganda, science fiction, epic battle sequences, and whimsical utopia (with, just perhaps, a few subtle hints of dystopia). Mayakovsky called the piece an "agitpoema," or long agitational poem (see the "1925" section of "I Myself"), stressing its propagandistic, call-to-arms content. The enormous air battle described in the first section, fought by the united forces of Red Europe and Asia against America, the last bastion of bourgeois capitalism, strongly recalls the fight between Ivan and Woodrow Wilson in the earlier poem "150,000,000." Here, too, the outcome is never really in doubt; the moment things get ugly for the Reds, Mayakovsky resorts to a deus ex machina resolution, cutting the tension in an almost comic way before the reader has a chance to prepare for the worst. Sections two and three are imbued with the dream of flight. The title of the poem—*Letaiushchii proletarii* in transliterated Russian—points to a phonetic link between the proletariat and the act of flying (this link is also the basis of several rhymes in the original), and Mayakovsky throughout the poem embraces flight as the answer to—or means of escape from—all the problems plaguing his country. Chief among these problems, at least for Mayakovsky, is his old nemesis, *byt* (the daily grind, conventional life, etc.); but strangely enough, the utopian future he envisions, while ostensibly and explicitly freed from *byt*, could also be seen as hopelessly submerged in it. This curious contradiction lends the buoyant second section some much-needed gravitas, even if the poet's playful inventiveness carries the day in the end. Such utopian fiction, by the way, contradicted Lef's stated views on the role of literature in Soviet society, so one can look at this work as an act of rebellion against those constraints by the poet's creative consciousness. (The poem's foreword can be seen as Mayakovsky's admission that its content flies in the face of Lef's beloved "literature of fact.")

Foreword

259 *The Truth . . . The News* The newspapers *Pravda* (*The Truth*) and *Izvestiia* (*The News*) were the two leading news organs and propaganda machines in the Soviet Union. Mayakovsky's plodding, redundant formula here is a forerunner to the more cynical version that would become popular in later Soviet times: "There's no news in *The Truth* and no truth in *The News*."

I. The War Soon to Come

260 *For a decade now* At the time of writing, ten years had passed since the outbreak of the First World War (6:533).

The Year 2125

261 *Aero-Rosta* Rosta was the Russian Telegraph Agency, where Mayakovsky worked on propaganda posters in the early 1920s.

Radio Meeting

264 *the mobile Comintern field rostrum* The Comintern was the international Communist organization dedicated to promoting workers' revolutions throughout the world. In the future Mayakovsky describes, they have apparently succeeded everywhere but in America.

Air Mobilization

266 *Pioneers and little Octobrists* Communist youth organizations popular in the Soviet Union.

267 *bourgooeys* My rendering of a (standard) colloquial and pejorative word for bourgeois or capitalist.

267 *Coolidges* As in "The Brooklyn Bridge," rhyme requires the mispronunciation of Coolidge's name, with the stress on the second syllable. This belittlement is compounded by Mayakovsky's characteristic pluralization of the proper noun.

The Enemy Attacks

276 *the Ku Klux Klan* Denouncing the racism of capitalist societies would become a staple of Soviet propaganda in years to come.

276   *a fascist flourish*   The right-facing swastika was adopted as a symbol by the Nazi Party in 1920, so that may very well be the flourish or symbol Mayakovsky has in mind (though he does not refer to it by name).

II. Daily Life in the Future

The Way It Is Now

292   *the Commission*   The Commission for the Improvement of Scholars' Living Conditions (KUBU in Russian) was involved in the rather complicated question of housing at the time (6:533).

Labor

298   *broths from Maggi cubes*   The Maggi brand bouillon cube was introduced in 1908, and the company exists to this day.

299   *Underwood*   A brand of typewriter (6:533).

Evening

308   *the Great Bear*   The constellation Ursa Major.

308   *Petrovsky Park*   A park in Moscow.

311   *Vinnitsa*   A city in Ukraine on the Southern Bug River.

312   *all the world's Chaliapins*   Fyodor Chaliapin (1873–1938) was one of the most famous opera singers of the twentieth century. Mayakovsky seems to have enjoyed the challenge of finding rhymes for Chaliapin's name (here he uses *naliapany:* "knocked off," "dashed off," etc.). See also "150,000,000."

312   *Art Theater . . : Ars*   Movie theaters in Moscow (6:533).

313   *from cobbler to tailor*   Both these professions were notorious among Russians for drinking; alcoholic cobblers and tailors are stock characters in classical Russian literature.

III. An Appeal

315   *O D V F*   The Society of Friends of the Air Force (6:533).

316   *the Khodynka*   An early airfield near Moscow (ibid).

Brown, Edward J. *Mayakovsky: A Poet in the Revolution*. Princeton, N.J.: Princeton University Press, 1973.

Cavanagh, Clare. "Whitman, Mayakovsky, and the Body Politic." In *Rereading Russian Poetry*, edited by Stephanie Sandler, 202–22. New Haven, Conn.: Yale University Press, 1999.

Gasparov, Mikhail. *Ocherk istorii russkogo stikha*. Moscow: Fortuna, 2002.

———. *Sovremennyi russkii stikh: Metrika i ritmika*. Moscow: Nauka, 1974.

Gorb, Bronislav. *Shut u trona revoliutsii: Vnutrennii siuzhet tvorchestva i zhizni poeta i aktera Serebrianogo veka Vladimira Maiakovskogo*. Moscow: Uliss-Media, 2001.

Jakobson, Roman. *Language in Literature*. Edited by Krystyna Pomorska and Stephen Rudy. Translated by Edward J. Brown. Cambridge, Mass.: Harvard University Press, 1987.

Janecek, Gerald. *The Look of Russian Literature: Avant-Garde Visual Experiments, 1900–1930*. Princeton, N. J.: Princeton University Press, 1984.

Karabchievskii, Iuri A. *Voskresenie Maiakovskogo: Filologicheskii roman. Esse*. Moscow: Russkie slovari, 2000.

Katanian, Vasilii A. *Maiakovskii: Khronika zhizni i deiatel'nosti*. 5th ed. Moscow: Sovetskii pisatel', 1985.

Katsis, Leonid F. *Vladimir Maiakovskii: Poet v intellektual'nom kontekste epokhi*. 2nd ed. Moscow: Rossiiskii gosudarstvennyi gumanitarnyi universitet, 2004.

Lawton, Anna, and Herbert Eagle, eds. *Words in Revolution: Russian Futurist Manifestoes 1912–1928*. Washington, D.C.: New Academia, 2005.

Lotman, Iuri. *O poetakh i poezii*. St. Petersburg: Iskusstvo–SPb, 2001.

Maiakovskii, Vladimir V. *Polnoe sobranie sochinenii v trinadtsati tomakh*. 13 vols. Moscow: Gosudarstvennoe izdatel'stvo khudozhestvennoi literatury, 1955–61.

Markov, Vladimir. *Russian Futurism: A History*. Washington, D.C.: New Academia, 2006.

Papernyi, Zinovii. *Poeticheskii obraz u Maiakovskogo*. Moscow: Izdatel'stvo Akademii nauk SSSR, 1961.

Pasternak, Boris. *Sobranie sochinenii v piati tomakh*. 5 vols. Moscow: Khudozhestvennaia literatura, 1991.

Pertsov, Viktor. *Maiakovskii: Zhizn' i tvorchestvo.* 3 vols. Moscow: Nauka, 1969–72.

Peterson, Dale. "Mayakovsky and Whitman: The Icon and the Mosaic." *Slavic Review* 28, no. 3 (1969): 416–25.

Shklovsky, Viktor B. *Theory of Prose.* Translated by Benjamin Sher. Normal, Ill.: Dalkey Archive Press, 1990.

Strizhneva, Svetlana, ed. *"V tom, chto umiraiu, ne vinite nikogo"? Sledstvennoe delo V. V. Maiakovskogo.* Moscow: Ellis Lak 2000, 2005.

Tsvetaeva, Marina. *Sobranie sochinenii v semi tomakh.* 7 vols. Moscow: Ellis Lak, 1994.

Tynianov, Iuri. *Arkhaisty i novatory.* Berlin: Priboi, 1929.

Vaiskopf, Mikhail. *Vo ves' logos: Religiia Maiakovskogo.* Moscow: Salamandra, 1997.

Vinokur, Grigorii. *Maiakovskii novator iazyka.* Moscow: Sovetskii pisatel', 1943.